Praise for **Capacity**

"One of the most frustrating components of building a small business is that the owner doesn't know how to build, grow, scale, and potentially sell the business. It's excruciating getting incremental growth year after year and having no idea how to show a Quantum Leap. Dustin Hillis has grown a business to $100 million. He understands recruiting, scale, and enterprise value. He understands hyper-scaling at a rapid rate. This book, *Capacity*, will show you step-by-step how you get out of the miserable zone of small and get to the scaling zone. I highly recommend *Capacity*. Get ready for hyper-growth with a laser-like focus."

—Coach Micheal Burt, Author, *Flip the Switch*,
and Founder, The Greatness Factory

"*Capacity* is a field guide in leadership and business growth, offering a concrete blend of strategic insight and personal wisdom. Dustin Hillis delivers a powerful, actionable road map for entrepreneurs and executives ready to scale their businesses to the next level. This book is a must-read for anyone serious about building something bigger than themselves."

—Matt Moore, Author, *Serial Griller*; Television Host;
and Serial Entrepreneur

"In *Capacity*, Dustin Hillis delivers a rare combination of practical strategy, inspiring vision, and battle-tested leadership principles. I've had the privilege of working alongside Dustin as he's led SafeSpace Global through transformational growth, and I've seen firsthand how the principles in this book create extraordinary results. If you're serious about scaling your business beyond your personal limits, this is the blueprint you've been waiting for."

—Scott M. Boruff, CEO and Chairman,
SafeSpace Global Corporation

"In *Capacity*, Dustin Hillis masterfully blends visionary leadership with practical strategies you can apply immediately. His stories are inspiring, his principles are timeless, and his insights will challenge you to dream bigger and lead with greater purpose. If you're serious about scaling your business and your life, this book is your blueprint."

—Jamie George, Author, *Love Well, Poets and Saints*,
and *The Thrivalist Handbook*

"Dustin Hillis doesn't just teach you how to build a bigger business—he shows you how to develop people into who they were meant to be. *Capacity* is more than a business book; it's a call to live with purpose, lead with integrity, and serve in a way that empowers others and multiplies impact. Just like a great song sticks with you, Dustin's words will keep playing in your head long after you've turned the last page."

—Mike Donehey, Author, *Finding God's Life for My Will*;
Speaker; and Cofounder, Tenth Avenue North

CAPACITY

Also by Dustin Hillis

Navigate: Selling the Way People Like to Buy

Navigate 2.0: Selling the Way People Like to Buy
(coauthored with Steve Reiner)

Redefining Possible: Proven Strategies to Break Belief Barriers and Create Your New Normal
(coauthored with Ron Alford)

CAPACITY

BUILDING YOUR BUSINESS BIGGER THAN YOU

DUSTIN HILLIS

MATT HOLT

Matt Holt Books
An Imprint of BenBella Books, Inc.
Dallas, TX

MATT HOLT ≣≣ BenBella

Matt Holt is an imprint of BenBella Books, Inc.
8080 N. Central Expressway
Suite 1700
Dallas, TX 75206
benbellabooks.com
Send feedback to feedback@benbellabooks.com

Matt Holt and *BenBella* are federally registered trademarks.

Printed in the United States of America
10 9 8 7 6 5 4 3 2 1

Library of Congress Control Number: 2025030811
ISBN 9781637748039 (hardcover)
ISBN 9781637748046 (electronic)

Editing by Lydia Choi
Copyediting by James Fraleigh
Proofreading by Jenny Bridges and Lisa Story
Indexing by WordCo Indexing Services, Inc.
Text design and composition by Jordan Koluch
Pillar illustration by Drew Robinson, Sport Design, Inc.
Cover design by Leigh Klemmer, Avaliis.com
Printed by Versa Press

I dedicate this book to two groups of people.

Group 1: Thank you to everyone who has ever believed in me. I am eternally grateful to everyone in my life who has shown faith in me, prayed for me, and lifted me up when I was down. Thank you to every team member who has ever joined a team where I was the leader. Your loyalty and belief in me will never be forgotten. Thank you to my family, who has believed in me through many ups and downs. Life has not been easy, but it keeps getting better. Having my family with me through all the storms is priceless. I love you all.

Group 2: Thank you to everyone who has told me, "You cannot do that," or doubted my capacity in any way. Growing up dyslexic, I was forced to learn how to get things done in a different way. Most people don't understand the processes I create or follow to achieve substantial goals. Because I don't necessarily do things the conventional way, they doubt my abilities and question my goals and leadership. This has served as fuel my whole life. Most of the goals I've set, few people believed I would achieve—so to all the skeptics out there ... thank you for the motivational fuel. Keep telling me what I cannot do. :)

Contents

The Backstory

You don't have time to read this book, and that's exactly why you need to read this book.

This book is a comprehensive guide to developing a strategy to scale your company to its potential. It is the toolkit you need to win back time, save wasted energy, and grow your capacity as an entrepreneur and/or leader.

Your capacity is defined as what you are capable of doing. "Capacity" as a term is most often used negatively—"I just don't have the capacity to do that." The goal of this book is to redefine how you think of the word "capacity" to be positive, such as, "I have unlimited capacity for where I choose to put my focus." I truly believe you are capable of doing much more than you currently can comprehend. The more you expand your belief of what your capacity is, the more you will be able to do. It all starts with you believing your capacity is unlimited.

I developed this sense of capacity over 25 years of experience in which I've had the somewhat rare opportunity to start off, after getting hurt playing college football, from the bottom as a straight-commission salesman, to cofounding a business that scaled to over 10 countries, and then to leading dozens of different businesses in a multitude of industries across the world as CEO of a large global conglomerate.

I am practicing all of the principles found in this book and testing my personal capacity daily. Currently, I am a global technology leader as the founder of All Things New Ventures, a sweat equity business that helps grow the value of businesses. I am also the president and chief strategy officer of SafeSpace Global Corporation (stock ticker SSGC), a publicly traded global multimodal AI company that helps save lives. We currently have over 50 team members and offices in Singapore, India, and Nashville and Knoxville, Tennessee. Additionally, I am the chief strategy officer of Tough Stump Technologies, a military and first-responder sUAV (drone) tracking and training technology company that helps save the lives of heroes. I am also the host of the *All Things New Ventures Podcast*. Plus, I've been authoring this book and speaking about and selling it as much as possible. And I've been married for 20 years to my beautiful boss babe wife, Kyah, and have a brilliant, entrepreneurial, cool 14-year-old daughter named Haven. I don't walk in the door at home on the phone. I eat dinner with the family most nights uninterrupted. I rarely miss a school play, sporting event, or anything else that's important to my daughter or wife. Without the tools found in this book, none of this would be possible.

Starting off at the ground floor as a straight-commission door-to-door salesman, I paid my own expenses and worked

80-plus hours a week during summer breaks in Alaska, Texas, and Missouri—all far away from the University of Tennessee, my college. I finished first out of 2,500 salespeople my first year and, in my fourth summer, broke the 150-plus-year-old sales record, earning over $100,000 in a 14-week summer—not bad for a college student's summer job in 2004.

Then I had to recruit other people to go do that job, which was arguably one of the hardest recruiting tasks there is: convincing college kids to move a thousand miles away from home and work on straight commission. My first team had eight team members, and leading them was much more difficult than breaking sales records solo. This was my first lesson on the challenge of *building a business bigger than myself*: **It is much easier to personally produce results than to motivate others to excel.**

Next, I created a business plan to start my own company, talking to specific people like Dave Ramsey and those at multinational corporate conglomerates (MCCs), looking at the options of bootstrapping it on my own, and weighing the options of taking on a corporate financing partner. Together with my partners, we built that company into a global consulting and coaching business that grew at 68% per year for 10 years in a row, making over $100 million in revenue through providing my services on a global scale with organizations from Fortune 500 companies to start-ups. I personally led the team that curated four different coaching curricula used with over 20,000 one-on-one coaching clients in more than a dozen countries, which has increased client incomes on average by over 40%.

Then I accepted an offer, after 10 years of running and

growing the coaching and consulting company, and employing over 150 coaches and 30 operations team members, to become CEO of the multinational corporate conglomerate (MCC) that our consulting business was part of. Upon becoming CEO, the MMC had 30 companies in the portfolio—half of them making money and half of them losing money, and all with a lot of problems that needed to be solved—and thousands of people under my leadership.

Fast-forward four years, and there were 20 successful companies: 5 new companies, and 15 of the old ones. Every one that reported to me was profitable and above budget.

After 20 years of dedicated growth and building this MCC, I moved on and started All Things New Ventures, where I partner with owners and entrepreneurs as an equity partner and help instill business systems to grow and scale. Part of the process is helping leaders evolve from being scrappy entrepreneurs to becoming true CEOs leading executive teams, while scaling their businesses to be worth $100 million and beyond.

After two years of operating All Things New Ventures and helping multiple companies grow their value tenfold and beyond, I was promoted to president of SafeSpace Global Corporation, the global leader in multimodal AI technology that helps save lives. When I started with SafeSpace, it was called Healthcare Integrated Technologies and was focused on the senior living sector. The stock was trading at $0.06, and the market cap was around $7 million. The team was comprised of a handful of part-time people, and there was no real focus on how to grow the core business. Ten months later, we raised over $10 million in our Friends & Family Round, changed our name to SafeSpace Global Corporation, and expanded our patented multimodal AI technology to schools, transportation, prisons, commercial real estate, and healthcare, as well as senior living. It's been gratifying to practice all of the strategies in this book once again by managing and running this global company. Meanwhile, I was also the chief strategy officer of Tough Stump Technologies, a rapidly growing drone technology tracking and training company for military and first responders, and chief strategy officer of Totally Mushrooms, which has the vision of being the US leader in fully integrated technology for growing and producing the highest-quality mushroom extracts for supplements—all while writing and selling this book.

Now, there are books out there on individual parts of executive strategy; you can find books on business development and sales strategy, as well as many others about marketing, legal, and financial strategy. But I struggled to find a comprehensive view of everything you need to do to go from being a bootstrapping entrepreneur to a high-functioning CEO. In other words, I saw a need for a guide on *how to grow your business bigger than you.* That's what this book is designed to help you do.

The reality is that what entrepreneurs deal with daily looks, feels, and sounds a lot different than what successful CEOs do—those with an executive team that report to them, to whom they can delegate high-level responsibilities and thus increase their own capacity. When it comes to transitioning from do-it-all entrepreneur to executive leader, most people don't even know where to start. Many successful founders ask me to help them with being too overloaded to grow their business. That is the first symptom of the deeper issue: **The inability to increase capacity is the beginning of burnout.**

Entrepreneurs often think they know what they need help with. They will say, "I need help with business development," or "I need help with raising money," or "I need help with increasing revenue." But they are often so focused on one problem that their mind hasn't expanded to the broader picture—that maybe the real problem is their lack of a comprehensive executive strategy. So they're asking for more of a Band-Aid for a symptom than the comprehensive cure they actually need. Such solutions are usually much more intricate and involved in the structure of the business than just "I need help with sales."

You might be thinking, *That's great, Dustin, but I don't have the time to develop and implement an executive strategy. I don't even have time to read this book. I'm too busy building a business and trying to keep up with the rest of my life.* Let me echo my opening sentence: If you don't have time to read this book, then you are exactly the person who needs to read this book the most.

You are the successful, growing entrepreneur or leader who needs to cross the bridge to being a true executive and CEO, and that bridge is executive strategy. You need a comprehensive executive strategy field guide to help you define and implement the 5 Strategic Pillars, the five strategies that you and your business need to *grow your business bigger than you*:

The 5 Strategic Pillars of Capacity:

1. Executive Strategy
2. Business Development Strategy
3. Marketing Strategy
4. Financial Strategy
5. Legal Strategy

If you want to scale your business to its potential, clarify your vision, find more time to do the most important things at work, do what you want in your personal life without sacrificing your business, and make a bigger impact in the world, then keep reading—this book is your best next step.

In each chapter of this executive strategy field guide, I'll introduce the main idea, give you an overview, share a story of how someone got it wrong and a story about someone who got it right, and then break the main idea down into its detailed components so you can understand how it works. Lastly, I'll offer some real-world applications and advice.

Let's start with the most important idea in this book: Executive Strategy.

Pillar 1

EXECUTIVE STRATEGY: DEFINING THE PATH TO SUCCESS

Executive Strategy is your compass, your map, your battle plan for creating more capacity. This is why Executive Strategy is the first of the 5 Strategic Pillars in this comprehensive field guide. **You should always be executing and refining your predesigned plan—your Executive Strategy. Do**

> **Your capacity is directly correlated to the strength of your systems.**

your thinking before the test, design your game plan before kickoff, prepare your battle plan before engaging the enemy, because that is when most wars are won: before a single shot is fired.

However, this is important: When defining and executing strategy, context is everything. There is no canned Executive Strategy formula that will work for everybody. Your Executive Strategy will be unique to you and your business, which is why most people don't like it, don't do it, and are no good at it. **Strategic thinking is hard work. Everybody wants the quick fix, the magic pill. Everybody wants to lose weight fast, but they don't want to go to the gym. Defining the path to success by sitting down and thinking through your Executive Strategy is the most important work you can do as a CEO.** This is the work we will do here in the First Strategic Pillar.

Executive Strategy is the compass that guides you as a leader, and over time, develops into a map. As you write down a plan, boil it down to a one-page document, and commence your Executive Strategy, a critical question will present itself: "Who?"

Who am I? What are my strengths and weaknesses as a leader?

Who does my company need me to be and not be?

Who should be doing which roles in the company?

Who are the other leaders in the company that can handle expanded roles?

Who is missing from the current team that I need to recruit? What roles need filling?

Who is going to be on my direct team? Who are my direct reports?

Who are the A+ people I can count on to get things done right across the entire organization?

Who are the strategic partners I can count on outside of
my full-time team members?
Who should be on my executive team?

The answers to these questions inform the people, delegation systems, and culture of your organization. However,
these questions can't be answered without organizing your
thoughts into strategic departments. The reason why Executive Strategy is so important is that it helps eliminate this
kind of deep thinking when you are in the battle and should
be taking action and getting things done. **You are doing
your thinking on the front end so you don't always have to
be making deep decisions on the fly; you'll have done the
work ahead of time.**
This kind of thinking is a high-skill activity—not everybody has the skill to put strategy together. It's also very hard
work, and many people just aren't willing to do it. They don't
have the willpower, the stamina, the work ethic, or the discipline to carve out the time, sit down, and prioritize modeling
a proper business strategy—a business plan—then commit
to refining the model over and over until it works. So not
only do you have to do it the first time—and most people
won't even start there—but then you have to refine it over
and over and over again. At a minimum, you should refine
your strategy annually, and if you're really good, you'll have
the flexibility to look at it quarterly. Once you really get it
dialed in, you can review it monthly. The most important
result from taking the time to create a world-class Executive
Strategy is to increase your capacity. Now is the time to build
both.

EXECUTIVE STRATEGY OVERVIEW

What exactly is Executive Strategy? Or, to put it another way, what are its major components? There are five structural elements to this Strategic Pillar:

1. Understanding Your Core Values and Motivation
2. Setting Clear, Achievable Goals with Time Frames
3. Aligning the Executive Team
4. Navigating the Market and Strategic Product Positioning
5. Adapting, Evolving, and Growing

First, every strong strategy is rooted in unshakable core values. What are the nonnegotiable principles that define your organization and drive motivation?

Second, goals should be ambitious yet achievable, serving as beacons that guide your every decision, and always attached to a time frame.

Third, a well-defined strategy is only effective if the entire executive team is in place and on board. This means finding the right people, establishing clear lines of communication, sharing a powerful vision, and creating a united front within your leadership team.

Fourth, understanding your market and product positioning is crucial. This involves not only recognizing opportunities and potential but also being aware of possible challenges and how to navigate them. As noted, context is everything.

Fifth, an executive strategy isn't set in stone; it's a living, breathing plan that must adapt to changing circumstances and evolving goals. This is why ongoing feedback and review processes for everything, up to and including your core Executive Strategy components, are so important.

As we dive deeper into these elements, remember that **a well-defined executive strategy is more than a plan; it's a commitment to a compelling vision, clarity on the game plan, and flexibility to achieve exponential growth. It's about charting a course that is uniquely yours, yet flexible enough to adapt to the unforeseen challenges and opportunities that lie ahead.**

The Imperative of a Well-Defined Executive Strategy

A business without a well-defined Executive Strategy lacks accountability. Everybody blames everybody else: "It's not my fault." "It's the owner's/operation's/marketing's/sales team's fault." "If I had more money, it would be better." "If I had more time, it would be right." "If I had more resources I could grow." People are playing the blame game and no one is actually connected to the reality of what the real problems are—or how to fix them. Nothing is aligned, everyone is pulling in different directions, the founder is probably doing too much, people are burning out or leaving—these are the kinds of things that happen when there is no Executive Strategy.

A good Executive Strategy starts with understanding roles and responsibilities: Who is supposed to be doing what? Then, when problems arise, you'll know who to hold accountable to identify the real problem, and then you can partner with them to fix it.

In the following sections, we'll dissect each of the major components of Executive Strategy, providing you with practical advice and strategies to establish a robust executive framework that propels your organization forward. First, though, I want you to see and feel what it looks like to get Executive Strategy wrong, and what it looks like when you get it right.

GETTING IT WRONG: THE WEWORK WAKE-UP CALL

On November 6, 2023, coworking space giant WeWork filed for Chapter 11 bankruptcy protection, months after its stock fell under $1.00 a share and risked being delisted from the New York Stock Exchange. Its April 2023 valuation was $360.9 million, down from $47 billion in 2019. Despite nearly $16 billion from Japanese multinational investing conglomerate SoftBank, WeWork's bankruptcy paperwork estimated their liabilities at somewhere between $10 billion and $50 billion.[1]

WeWork seemingly had everything: a charismatic, ambitious founder in Adam Neumann; SoftBank's deep pockets backing them; plenty of Silicon Valley buzz; broad-based investor confidence; a jump on the competition; a powerful brand. How did it all go so wrong?

The truth is, WeWork was a train wreck with no Executive Strategy. It did have an eccentric leader with a real vision, but he had no true Executive Strategy. A hell of a salesman, Neumann nevertheless personified everything I despise about the stereotypical used-car dealer. I've been on a mission for the past 20 years to help undo that way of thinking for people, teaching them to sell ethically, honestly, and without shortcuts. That is the right way to sell. The best salespeople in the world are the ones who listen, ask questions, find people's needs, and help them with a solution.

Salespeople can be world-changing servants, changing peoples' lives for good. Neumann, however, was self-serving, and it seemed like all he cared about was making money, sex, drugs, and rock 'n' roll—quite literally. He sold all those investors a bill of goods that wasn't based in reality.

The WeWork story shows us how money and investors will only get you so far in fixing problems. People think that there's all this sophistication in how investors think, but sometimes it's just the person that's the most charismatic, that says the right things, who gets the money. The best investors, though, are the ones that look at a candidate company's Executive Strategy.

In the documentary based on the WeWork trainwreck, a few people turned Neumann down when he asked them to invest in his vision. The documentary seemed to characterize these people as the bad guys, but the reality is, those were really the smart people, because Neumann had no strategy. It was a dream, and he was just BS-ing everybody the whole time. The character that came in and ultimately became the CEO who tried to save the company was the first guy that actually had a strategy.

As the story unfolds, the new CEO asks questions like, "Wait, what's our strategy here? What's our price point? What's our structure? How's this working?" He makes everyone get rid of all the Don Julio 1942 tequila and actually holds structured meetings. In the documentary, it feels as though he's ruining the culture. The culture was already ruined, though, because there was no Executive Strategy, and without Executive Strategy, culture devolves into the lowest common denominator. Ultimately, it was too little, too late, because they should have had an Executive Strategy from the beginning, one based on clearly articulated core values driving goals and shaping the executive team and the culture, enabling the company to navigate an ever-changing market by adapting and evolving according to the strategy. Without that Executive Strategy, no amount of brilliance, charisma, or investment could have saved WeWork, regardless of what "world-changing" vision Adam Neumann was selling.

GETTING IT RIGHT: CHICK-FIL-A'S STRATEGY AND CULTURE

Chick-fil-A has a goal: to be the most caring company in the world. It's also an outstanding success in virtually every way you can measure a business. By 2002, 35 years into its existence, Chick-fil-A had topped $1 billion in sales. By 2017, its revenue was over $2.5 billion. Five years later, in 2022, it exceeded $6 billion in revenue on almost $19 billion in sales. The chain's unstoppable growth is all the more amazing because it is privately owned, having never issued stock to the public. Instead, Chick-fil-A achieved this through total strategic and cultural alignment, from its founding family to their top executives and all the way down.

The core values, purpose, and culture of Chick-fil-A are

communicated at every level of the company, from the very top to their newest trainees. Its founder, S. Truett Cathy, established the business on Biblical principles, which he believed to be good business principles as well. Chick-fil-A's Corporate Purpose has guided all that it does since 1967, keeping this Purpose "front and center," because its owners believe it helps them to steward their business and their work to positively influence everyone they meet: "To glorify God by being a faithful steward of all that is entrusted to us. To have a positive influence on all who come in contact with Chick-fil-A."[2] To do this, they emphasize creating a caring culture both at their Support Center and in restaurants, where honor, dignity, and respect are paramount.

Chick-fil-A values serving others, teamwork, purpose-driven work, and innovation. Its workplace culture includes closing on Sundays for rest and family time. The company encourages work–life balance and provides amenities like childcare services. To ensure that these values reach every corner of their organization, Chick-fil-A holds regular team meetings, optional devotions, innovation sessions, and other activities. It prioritizes staying connected on every level through a variety of meetings, talks, and annual conferences.

I had the pleasure of visiting Chick-fil-A's headquarters and interviewing Chairman Dan Cathy, son of S. Truett Cathy, several years ago. It was raining that day in Georgia, yet the guard at the gate was standing outside in a raincoat and had the biggest smile on his face that you've ever seen. When I rolled down my window, he said, "You must be Dustin Hillis."

And I said, "Yes, I am."

He said, "Mr. Cathy is so excited to meet with you today. You just have a great day. And can I get a high five?"

I said, "Yeah, you can." And he gave me a high five.

And so I drove onto their beautiful campus, thinking, *That's the greatest welcome from a guard—in the rain—that I've ever had in my entire life.* I parked, walked up to the door, and started to shake the rain off. The lady sitting at the front desk jumped up when she saw me, ran around the desk, swung the door open before I got a chance to touch the handle, and said, "Welcome to Chick-fil-A. You must be Dustin Hillis."

And I said, "Well, yes, I am."

"Come on in. Dry off. Mr. Cathy's excited to meet you," she replied. "In the meantime, why don't you take a tour of our little mini-museum here?" (They have the original Batmobile in the lobby of Chick-fil-A, it turns out.)

After a look at the museum, I sat down, already blown away. I had only met the guard and the front desk worker, and this was already the coolest company I had ever seen. Then a vice president came and met me, gave me a similar greeting, and shook my hand. He was the warmest, friendliest, nicest guy, and knew me by name. "Hello, Mr. Hillis— you want a tour? Mr. Cathy's not going to be able to meet us until the prayer breakfast in an hour, but I can give you a tour of the facility." So he gave me a tour, and as we walked down the hall, every single person I met made the time to make eye contact and say, "Hello, we're glad you're here." I had a visitor badge on, so they all knew to greet me. It was unbelievable. Even the rooms we went to were magnificent—all of them different and creative, and nothing that stank of corporate malarkey whatsoever.

Dan found me after the prayer meeting and said, "Okay, let's go have some breakfast and meet right over there." I began to put on my coat, but by the time I turned around, he had already taken off and was far away from me. There were a bunch of people moving around, too, getting between us. So, like a football player, I took off running, and I was juking and dodging people, full-on running to catch him. I was out of breath when I caught him, right before we walked down a set of stairs.

He looked at me out of the corner of his eye and kind of smiled before heading down the stairs. I thought, *That was weird. Was he trying to lose me?* As we sat down at the bottom of the stairs, his pen rolled off the desk, and I bent down to pick it up and hand it to him.

Finally, he asked, "So, what questions do you have for me?" I had a notepad, and I was very excited to interview him.

I said, "Well, thanks for meeting with me. Your culture and every Chick-fil-A I go to is amazing. How do you hire such good people?"

He laughed and said, "Well, I actually did part of our interview process with you this morning."

"Well, what are you talking about?"

"We actually completely took the corporate recruiting handbook and threw it out the window, and we created our own," he said. "We wanted to test people for real-life things that we look for in a store operator or team member during the interview."

"I'm intrigued," I replied. "Tell me what you do."

"When someone comes into the interview," Dan explained, "they walk in the main door, and we strategically put the interview room as far away from the check-in door as possible. Then we put a seat right next to the check-in. So if you are interviewing, you sign in and you sit down and they call your interviewer. Your interviewer comes and shakes your hand and says, 'Good to meet you. Right this way.'

"And they turn around, and they're trained to intentionally walk as fast as humanly possible away from you to the interview room, which is a pretty long walk away. And they're actually paying attention to how fast you get up and how fast you follow them. Are you too cool to run to catch somebody? Is your energy level not high enough to walk fast to keep up with somebody? And that's the first part of the interview."

"So you did that to me when we left the meeting?" I asked.

Dan replied, "Honestly, I just do it naturally now. I do it to everyone. But, yeah, I guess I did, but I didn't mean to."

"Well, you definitely smoked out of there, and I had to run to catch you," I said.

Dan laughed, then said, "The second test I actually did do. As soon as you sit down, we knock our pen underneath the table as far as we can. And part of the interview is, are you willing to get on your hands and knees and crawl under the table and get the pen and hand it to the interviewer? Because if you're willing to do that, then if you're managing a store, you'll be willing to crawl underneath that table and get the paper that is underneath the table, versus walking by and not picking it up."

And it occurred to me that day that this is the level of

thinking of a company like Chick-fil-A versus its competitors. I like the chicken at Bojangles, for instance, but every time I go there, there's paper on the floor and the service is inconsistent. If there is a Bojangles right next to a Chick-fil-A, 100% of the time I'm going to the Chick-fil-A. I might even like the chicken at Bojangles better, but the fact that I know it's going to be clean, I know the service is going to be stellar and timely—that's what makes the difference. So the quality of that interview process and the quality of their people and their culture is what differentiates Chick-fil-A from its competitors. The company has a certain culture, and that culture arises from its people, but it got those people because of certain predesigned processes, such as interviewing. Those processes come from thinking and planning, both of which are a result of its strategic vision—its Executive Strategy.

Dan shared with me that Chick-fil-A's production per store is double that of the number-two competitor in the world. Its revenue, profit per store, is literally double the second-place company. And by the way, its competitors are open seven days a week, and Chick-fil-A is open for six. Its competition has another whole day to sell more, but Chick-fil-A still does twice the number two's average store revenue.

Chick-fil-A started with vision, then corporate strategy, which then permeated into its culture. Strategy becomes culture over time. It also has long-term goals and a plan to get there. Truett Cathy is said to have famously stated, many years ago, "Thirty years from now, we're going to be the number one fast food restaurant in America."

And he got it right.

BREAKDOWN: EXECUTIVE STRATEGY

This chapter is dedicated to helping you lay a foundation for your Executive Strategy, as I've been able to do in a variety of settings in my career, and as Chick-fil-A has done so successfully over nearly six decades. Executive Strategy is about defining your path, aligning your team, and setting a course for sustainable success. Let's explore how to create a well-defined Executive Strategy that not only drives growth but also fosters a culture of excellence and innovation. We'll do this through understanding your core values; setting clear, achievable goals; recruiting and aligning your executive team; navigating the market; and adapting and evolving as you grow.

1. Understanding Your Core Values and Motivation

Every strong strategy is rooted in unshakable core values. Ask yourself: "What are the nonnegotiable principles that define our organization?"

Many consultants and books in the business world focus on the importance of core values. Why do so many people talk about core values? Because they're incredibly important. This concept is not unique, but I'd be remiss not to mention its importance. The reason whole consulting firms are built just to help you establish your core values is that, if you get those right, a lot of other things fall into place. Conversely, if you get them wrong, it can mess up a lot of things.

Your core values are your driving force. They should drive your decision-making. If Executive Strategy is your brain, core values are your heart. Many people have spoken and written about core values: Stephen Covey, Tony Robbins, Zig Ziglar. They talk about mission, vision, and values. You have to have all three, and they shouldn't remain stagnant or frozen in time. I prefer establishing the mission first, values second, and vision third.

Who are we? Why do we do what we do? And where are we going?

When working with a new business, the first thing I tend to do is a full day, or sometimes two days, of just helping companies establish these three things:

1. Why do we do what we do? / What is our mission?
2. Who are we? / What are our core values?
3. Where are we going? / What is our vision?

By the time you've built out a well-defined mission, vision, and values, they usually all feel very motivating and provide clarity and direction. The key from my perspective is helping a business create a one-page document that encompasses all of those elements, and then forcing them to act on it, to make it central to everything they do. Most of the time we have to force it, because people will never really roll it out otherwise. It's amazing—companies will spend $10,000 for a consultant like me to spend a day with them, and then if you ask them six months later, "Hey, where is the one-pager? How was the rollout?" many times it hasn't happened. Because of this reality, you have to open every meeting by reading the one-pager out loud. You have to frame it and put it on everybody's desk.

Establishing core values cannot be a one-time thing, which is what a lot of companies end up doing. The executive team has to read it in every one of its meetings. Then, at least monthly, a great exercise is to go through every single line of the one-pager and ask, "Are we doing it?" You can also coach your ground-level team and say, "If any of our leaders are violating any of the core values that are in this document, you have complete permission to meet with that leader and hold them to it. Or, if you're scared, you come meet with me as the CEO, and we will handle it together." It's that important.

As a CEO, I would help people do this. I also train other CEOs to do this, to say, "What I want you to do is quote the aspect of our creed, vision, value statement, purpose statement. I want you to quote it, and then tell me what your leader did that didn't align with our core values." And then, when the ground-level people have permission to hold themselves and the leadership accountable to the mission, vision, and values, it all starts to become real. Everybody starts paying attention to what is actually in that one-pager. Some organizations decide on a "three times and you're out" rule. I've had companies use the one-pager as a guide for when it's the right time for firing people: "If you violate one of these core values three times, this isn't the right home for you."

Once you have your core values in place, people are buying in, and there is understanding from top to bottom about those values, everything else can start to fall in place.

This first step of understanding your core values is critical in developing your Executive Strategy, but it's not the only step.

2. Setting Clear, Achievable Goals with Time Frames

Your goals should be ambitious, clear, and achievable, serving as beacons that guide every decision you make. Typically, your financials should guide your goals, because your business plan will roll up into your P&L, which should reflect your budget, which encompasses your goals. You should have a well-put-together financial statement and a disciplined financial review, every single month, no matter what, with your C-suite—your leaders—looking at the financials together in a meaningful way. In other words: Do you have a well-organized monthly financial review?

Here's what a financial review should look like. First, it should actually exist (and you would be shocked at how rare this is). On the outside, people may think, *Oh, what a cool product, what a great company, what a great leader.* But the reality could be that, behind the scenes, no one's communicating with each other. Sales has no idea what Marketing is doing. Marketing has no idea what Operations is doing. Operations has no idea what Manufacturing is doing. All the vendors are completely disorganized. Payments are maybe going out on time, maybe not. Payroll is a mess, and everybody's just barely surviving.

I would say a majority of businesses are functioning that way. With this in mind, schedule a monthly financial review with your executive team every month, no matter what! This is the first step in ensuring your goals will increase your capacity.

Second, review the financials. Typically, your financial professional—CFO, controller, or accountant—should put a monthly P&L, cash balance sheet, and executive summary into a financial packet to review every month. Let this professional lead the meeting and walk all the stakeholders through the state of the union from the prior month. If you do not have a CFO, controller, or other financial professional on your executive team . . . get one! This is one of the most critical roles in your business. Most of the time the entrepreneur, rainmaker, and/or CEO does not make the best CFO. You need someone with an actual finance degree, preferably a CPA.

Third, take time for strategy. Working sessions are the best sessions. Don't walk past a problem just to "stay on agenda." Ask questions, dig into errors and fix them, pick up the phone and call people about a problem you see in the numbers during the financial review. Get work done and be productive. That being said, don't hijack the meeting. You still need to get through the financials and see all of the numbers your financial professional put together. If a problem you identify will take more than five minutes to properly address, schedule another meeting to solve it.

Corporate Planning & Executive Team Structure

Do you understand proper corporate planning and executive team structure? Note that you could have only five people on your team and still create a corporate structure. Just call it an "executive team" if you don't like the word "corporate." Who is on your executive team? And does everyone on this team have a role definition and job description? Does the CEO also have a role definition and job description? Most CEOs do not. You know why? They're probably the founder of the company. *Why would I have a job description?*, they think. *I'm the boss. I just do whatever I want.* Well, good luck growing a substantial company without a job description and a role definition as a CEO. Clearly defining those things is actually one of the healthiest things you can do as the leader. Then, once you define the CEO's role and job (and if they're the founder, they will probably assemble this only begrudgingly), you can do likewise down the whole C-suite. Without the structure of job descriptions, you can't reach your goals. First roles, then goals.

So you could have a CFO, COO, CMO, and CSO (chief strategy officer—this is how I function with a lot of the companies that are part of All Things New Ventures) as part of the C-suite, along with various other roles. You can establish presidents, VPs of HR, chief revenue officers, chief technology officers, chief information officers, and more. A lot of people don't know the difference between a CTO and a CIO, but big-enough companies need both. This might seem a little in the weeds here, but these are good examples of how much structure an organization can have.

Now, of course, if you're a company doing $100,000 a year, you might have two people in that structure, and that's okay. But even identifying these two people as your executive team, and creating the vision for what your company will be, is where the power comes from. That vision is what you as the leader will manifest your company into becoming. I believe the fact that a leader is willing to create a vision is what actually makes it become a reality.

For instance, the professional coaching business I co-founded did $300,000 in revenue its first year. That was pretty good, but I led the team that built the company's infrastructure, compensation plan, and budget for that next year as if we were going to do a million dollars. We budgeted as if we had the money and the people to backfill a structure that didn't even exist yet. We fully anticipated we were going to hit a million . . . which we did the next year! Ultimately, by focusing on the company's vision and goals and properly aligning the executive structure, that business grew to over $20 million in annual revenue and had a full executive team running it.

Businesses don't accidentally get to be million-dollar operations; at some point they need structure to grow. The difference between an entrepreneur and a CEO is the latter has a defined role, an actual job description, which should include leading other executives. A CEO shouldn't be the "Chief" of just themselves. By contrast, the entrepreneur does everything. They are the CEO and the chief bottle washer on the same day. But at some point, the entrepreneur can only take it so far by themselves, and they must have a team.

At first, they'll hire a generalist to do everything else they can't do. "I'm going to do this one thing—you do the other thing, and then let's go." As outlined in Gino Wickman's Entrepreneurial Operating System (EOS), many times, a Visionary entrepreneur just happens to find an Integrator—Steve Jobs and Steve Wozniak, for example—and forms a great partnership. If you are intentional, you can take the time to think, *I'm a Visionary, I need an Integrator.* Or you have two Visionaries, and sometimes they complement each other. While this can be powerful, too often they'll clash with each other and either one steps down or the company suffers.

At a certain point, the need to form a corporate plan and executive structure becomes inevitable. I think you can get there a lot faster if you read a book like this and realize, *Oh, what if I just went ahead and thought about this now? What if I went ahead and put a five-year business plan together? What if I went ahead and just let my mind expand, and I did the hard work of thinking about what the business would look like? What would the structure look like? What is even possible? What am I truly capable of as a leader? Have I ever really achieved my capacity?* That's what this book is going to help you with.

Now there are some founders—maybe 10% or fewer—that get lucky and succeed with no Executive Strategy, who just happen to be the right people at the right time with the right resources, and Lady Luck finds them. For example, Jed Clampett walked into his backyard to hunt a raccoon, missed the shot, but struck gold. Black gold, that is. You could be the Clampetts and just get lucky and not need an Executive Strategy, or instead, you could be a business professional, put a strategy together, and craft a vision for what that strategy should look like. Then you manifest the business model into reality. But it starts with the vision first, then the structure right behind. The structure is necessary for pursuing your goals. (And they must be SMART goals; more on that in a bit.)

As you establish a budget, a five-year business plan that ultimately gets rolled up in the financials, and your structure, make sure you take the time to think of what's possible. Most people set goals based on what they've already done. To me, that's silly, because, as Einstein is often credited as saying, "If you do what you've always done, you're going to get what you've always gotten."

That truth rings in my ears when I meet people who, when sharing their next year's goal, admit they're not only basing it on the previous year but also that they've been doing that for ten years . . . then wonder why they're doing $200,000 in revenue and barely paying the bills. And they're always saying, "Well, this is what we did last year, and this is what we did three years ago. And remember five years ago, we had that one really good customer, and we made an extra 2%?" But it just never scales. If you want to scale, you need a structure that enables you to do more than you've done in the past.

If you want to have a growth structure, you must be willing to do the work. Think of a bigger vision. And what will fuel that bigger vision is understanding what is possible. The best entrepreneurs out there are people like Elon Musk, where

> "If you do what you've always done, you're going to get what you've always gotten."

the thought probably never even crosses his mind: *What have I done?* All he's thinking about is, *What are we not doing yet?* That's why I draw inspiration from Elon Musk. He pushes me to think, *Well, if that one guy can do what he's doing, I can at least do one-tenth of what he's doing, because he's a human being and I'm a human being. We have the same amount of time in the day.* Now, he's probably smarter than me, and he's an actual genius, but one thing that makes him a genius is his mindset on how he thinks about what is possible.

So **if you want to scale, you must have structure. If you want structure, you must have a bigger vision. If you want a bigger vision, you must ask: What is possible?** But structure, vision, and what's possible must be articulated as clear, achievable goals: SMART goals.

SMART goals are:

Specific (vs. too general)
Measurable (vs. intangible)
Achievable (vs. pie in the sky)
Relevant (and Reviewed) (vs. random or unrelated to your vision and mission, and never revisited)
Time Bound (vs. open ended)

For example, "Get in better shape and run faster" is *not* a SMART goal. But having a fitness goal of running a six-minute mile by the end of the year, which you review every day, compare to your current nine-minute pace, and work toward by running three times a week and consulting a running coach on technique and training schedules, *is* a SMART goal.

Once you have your vision and understand what's possible at the top level of your organization, then you can say, "All right, over the next five years, here's what I think we can actually do," and you can let your mind go to work. Crucially, however, you cannot plan forward from today; you have to plan backwards from five years in the future. When you are casting a five-year business plan, if you get stuck on a "today problem," you will never have a future maximum po-tential. You will stop yourself before you even get started. In other words, dream the biggest possible goal five years down the line, and then reverse-engineer from there.

People don't do this because they cannot get past the problems they're dealing with today. My daughter likes to say to my wife, when she brings up some issue related to why she won't be able to do something, "Well, that's a 'future-you' problem, not a 'today-you' problem." It's kind of hilarious, because so much of why we don't do things or don't think something is possible is that we're thinking into the future— of problems we're *going* to have—but we're experiencing it today. So, we spend our time trying to solve those "tomorrow problems" today in our minds, and never get down to the business of setting and pursuing our goals.

Once you have your five-year goals, you can reverse-engineer those into a five-year business plan. That plan will let you start forecasting based on what the revenue is going to be. So many people are scared stupid to set a big, hairy, audacious goal: They fear failure, the unknown, and proba-bly even success. But if you can take that part of your brain, lock it in a cage, throw away the key, and not let yourself live in that fear, only letting your brain flow into what's possible, then you can set a five-year forecast and start asking:

- How much revenue and profit will we be producing in five years?
- How am I going to get there?
- Who's going to help me get there?
- What does the product mix look like?

- What is the price point?
- What positions do I need?
- What infrastructure do I need?
- How much money do I need?

Once you've aligned your vision and goals using the structure of your top people, their roles, and a five-year plan, you can start answering all those questions.

Another key question then arises: "How will the business evolve year over year?" Again, start from the future vision and work backwards, year after year, until you get to the present day. One example of a big dream might be to think, *In five years, I could have a $100 million business. We're going to be in every state in America. We're going to be in 12 different countries.* To do that, you're probably going to need a distribution center and a whole team of people. If you think, *I'm going to have online sales going,* then what follows is, *I'm probably going to need an entire IT department.* And what follows that might be, *I'll need an entire sales team. I'll need an inbound team taking up the leads. I'll need an outbound team handling national accounts.*

For a $100 million company that looks like this in five years, year four revenue is probably going to be some smaller percentage of that. Year three is going to be an even smaller percentage of that. Year two, another, still smaller percentage. So for year one, you'll need to ask yourself, *What do I think this year could be?* Let's say the previous actual year, you did $100,000 and it's you and three other people. Start with the goal of a million dollars and a 10% profit. Just getting your business to $1 million in revenue and profitability is a milestone most people never reach. If you drive down the road, 90% of the businesses you drive by are not doing a million dollars in revenue or at 10% EBITDA profitability. Here's what's interesting: **It's harder to take your business from nothing to $1 million and have a 10% EBITDA than it is to grow your business from a million to $10 million and maintain your margins.**

The things that it takes to get to $10 million are not the same things that it takes to get from $10 million to $100 million. You must be constantly learning. What got you from $1 million to $10 million is going to be completely different from what gets you from $10 million to $20 million. Then, what gets you from $20 million to $50 million is going to be different from $50 million to $100 million. You must be coachable. You must learn. Then you will grow.

3. Aligning the Executive Team

Before you can align the executive team, you have to understand it. Take the time to get to know the executive team members, especially if you're a new leader, you've just been promoted, you inherited the team, or you've just never taken the time to understand them. Maybe you've been in your position for a while, but you've been busy being an entrepreneur, you haven't yet considered team alignment, and you've just been telling people what to do—because you're paying them. That's different from aligning them as an executive team.

Executive team alignment means people have common goals and a common vision. Once everyone has bought

into the company vision and mission, and taken owner-ship of the company to the point where they feel like it's their own, that's when you have team alignment. But how do you get there?

First, as an old but true saying goes: **People don't care how much you know until they know how much you care. The way that a team member spells "care" is "T-I-M-E."** A lot of leaders think, *Oh, you know, my team knows I care about them because I pay them and because I tell them they're great and, you know, we have an annual Christmas party, and I tell funny jokes and I buy their beer.* Every leader in the world should be doing those things as a bare minimum any-way, but most team members don't equate those instances to you caring about them. However, if you're willing to invest an hour a week with every direct report one-on-one, and fully immerse yourself in that hour to understand who they are, what they value, what their motivations are—and figure out why they're there—then you'll start to really understand them. It's amazing how many leaders don't know why every team member that's on their team is physically there.

Then, learn what each team member's goals are. Most leaders don't know this either. Once you know why they are working with you and what their goals are, get to know them as individuals. Who's in their family? What do they enjoy doing? What motivates them? These are all critically import-ant things for a leader to know before attempting to align the team. This goes both ways; sharing about yourself with each team member, and being reasonably transparent, makes these relationships mutual. Building a relationship goes be-yond having rapport; most leaders stop at rapport and don't build true relationships with their teams. **My dad taught me that you can take somebody to breakfast, and they'll do a job for you. You can take somebody to lunch, and they'll work for you for a long time. But if you go with somebody and their spouse to dinner, especially at either party's house, you will have someone that buys into the mission and will want to work with you for a lifetime.**

Doing things socially with people and taking time within the work week to meet with them should not be just a one-time occurrence. Assign each person a spot in your schedule to meet with them one-on-one so you can hear what's going on. Give them an opportunity to celebrate good news and work on any problems they have. That time is what people value and how they know you care. If you do all those things, you'll have a team that knows you care. They also have to see you take action on feedback that was given, actually implement the feedback, and change as a leader.

If a member of your team gives you constructive feedback about yourself, don't get defensive; listen, take ownership of what you can, and then change. If they give you ideas for the company, and you actually enact them, the team will definitely see that. **When things go right, ensure it's the team that did it. When things go wrong, show it's the leader's fault.** The more your team sees you falling on the sword, even though it might have been their fault—if you publicly say, as the leader, "Hey, I'm taking ownership of this, I could have done better"—the more deposits you will make into people's "emotional bank accounts." And inevitably, as a leader, you will have to make a withdrawal at some point, such as when you're asking the team to get aligned.

People have a kind of natural resistance to team alignment. But when done right, they can become harmonious, like orchestrating a band to be in tune and in sync. A team that lacks alignment is like a band playing whatever the hell they want all at the same time, and it sounds like chaos. That's why the most unsuccessful companies are in chaos: People are frustrated and just doing a job to get a paycheck, because that lack of team alignment creates subterfuge, silos, dissension, and division.

Even the word "division" can subconsciously affect alignment. One thing we did years ago as a company for the four divisions in our consulting firm was to change the name from "division" to "business unit." We went from one company with four divisions to one company with four business units, and just that semantic idea alone is the type of thing that can go a long way—we can now assert, "We just don't have division within our company."

But how, practically, do you get everyone on the same page? Usually, you need about two days to get the entire executive team together. I do this any time I'm involved in helping a company grow.

How to Organize a Two-Day Executive Team Meeting

The most important step in a successful Executive Team meeting is making sure everybody is there in attendance. Make sure to include the executive leaders of every department—Operations, Accounting, Sales, Marketing, Legal, HR—in the same room for both days.

The leader's job is to set the agenda. What's the agenda? Who is speaking on the agenda? What time frames do you have allocated for each part? Here is an example:

Day 1:

- 9:00 AM–9:30 AM: Welcome and review mission, vision, and values (CEO)
- 9:30 AM–10:30 AM: General overview of the company, introduce new team members, and company updates (President)
- 10:30 AM–12:00 PM: Review goals and game plan for the year (CFO)
- 12:00 PM–1:00 PM: Lunch
- 1:00 PM– 5:00 PM: SWOT analysis [a breakdown of how to do a SWOT analysis is below]
- 6:00 PM– 8:00 PM: Executive Team dinner

Day 2:

- 9:00 AM–9:30 AM: Review of Day 1 and SWOT (COO)
- 9:30 AM–12:00 PM: Departmental Review and Strategy Sessions:
    - 9:30 AM–10:00 AM: Operations Strategy (COO)
    - 10:00 AM–10:30 AM: Business Development Strategy (CSO)
    - 10:30 AM–11:00 AM: Marketing Strategy (CMO)
    - 11:00 AM–11:30 AM: Financial Strategy (CFO)
    - 11:30 AM – 12:00 PM: Legal Strategy (GC)
- 12:00 PM–1:00 PM: Vendor Sponsored Lunch
- 1:00 PM–2:00 PM: Budget Review (CFO)
- 2:00 PM–4:00 PM: Goal Setting (CEO)
- 4:00 PM–5:00 PM: Q&A & Send-off

How to Do a SWOT Analysis

Set the stage for the SWOT section of the meeting where the entire team participates. List it in front of them, if you can, with notes or a projector, following each part of SWOT:

- What are our Strengths?
- What are our Weaknesses?
- What are our Opportunities?
- What are our Threats?

What's funny is that a lot of times, the CEO is the one who talks the most and tries to answer the questions. I often have to tell them, "I know what *you* think. Let's hear what *they* think." And it gets really good once everyone starts talking.

Getting everyone talking is crucial, because getting the team bought into the feedback loop of the SWOT allows them to take ownership—this also allows them to feel heard. A SWOT analysis is perfect for increasing trust, because it builds the unity of what everybody thinks, even the "strength" aspect of it. To have everybody talk about what their company's strengths are provides a lot of value: how to leverage and maximize strengths, increase confidence and morale, and build buy-in.

When you get to "weaknesses" in the SWOT analysis, you might need to prepare your team for how they should react to this phase. Say, "The purpose of this is not to be negative, but to be constructive. So, whatever we talk about here, we're saying this with a constructive mindset. It's okay to admit these are our weaknesses with a constructive mind-set, because we're going to put together solutions to fix these weaknesses."

Discussing your company's weaknesses is not a wine-and-cheese event, it's a reality check. People typically have a lot of things to say in this category, but as the leader, don't try to solve the problem during the exercise. Just write down what the team has to say, ask questions, and avoid being defensive. A lot of times, team members will naturally say what the opportunities and threats are, even without your prompting. If and when this happens, just roll with it. Write down what they say in the Opportunities or Threats section of the analysis. Then, after the discussion of weaknesses, you can explore what they think the opportunities are. Another goal of reviewing weaknesses is also to find opportunities, so take a lot of notes during the weakness phase, and ensure everybody has the chance to openly discuss what they think the biggest opportunities are. This gives rise to follow-ups like, "What are the things we can do about it?" It's how you maximize your strengths, minimize your weaknesses, ex-ploit your opportunities, and eliminate your threats.

With threats, sometimes a bogey comes from left field that you had no idea was out there, that somebody in a given de-partment sees, and they say, for instance, "Did you know our vendor is creating an exact competitor of what we're doing?" And you can say, "No, we did not. Please tell us more." In a sense, what you are really doing is crowdsourcing wisdom.

Sadly, few managers do this kind of thing—which is a shame, as I've yet to see one of these sessions where the team didn't absolutely love it, because by the end, they really feel heard. But you don't stop there; that's the first day, and on the second day you reconvene.

For day two, I like to talk through a goal-setting overview with the executive team before they break off into individual groups to talk about creating team alignment. Usually if you're training a group of people on setting goals, the first thing you must do is break down the mental barriers that stop them from wanting to commit to writing goals down.

Even quasi-successful people tend to have a hard time writing down a SMART goal—specific, measurable, attainable, relevant (and reviewed), with an actual timeframe. So, we teach them a SMART goal-setting framework. Instead of saying,

> **Setting a time frame is the difference between a goal and a dream.**

"I'm going to lose weight," you say, "I'm going to lose ten pounds, I'm going to weigh myself every single day, and I'm going to tell somebody else about it." As I mentioned, "reviewed" means you actually revisit it with some frequency to ensure it's still relevant to your vision and mission. Setting a time frame is the difference between a goal and a dream.

If you do all of this when people are setting goals, the odds are high that they will achieve their goals! I tell people, "This is great to do in your life, but let's do it as a team now. Let's get together with our departments, and let's talk about the things in this SWOT analysis we can do to put a strategic alignment plan together for the year." What points of improvement can each person take accountability for? Now that we have heard everyone's point of view and we feel safe talking about this stuff, where do we ask everybody else for help? What is it we want to do? Very rarely do you find that teams have ever done anything like this.

Give them about an hour to complete this task, and walk around to ensure they're doing it. Usually, you put a leader in each group. You have the Operations leaders, the Marketing leaders, and the Sales leaders, depending on how big your organization is. Sometimes it's just two groups: Operations, Sales, whatever business groups you have.

This leadership strategy meeting should be an annual meeting. Make sure leadership has already been prepared for this annual two-day summit. You need to say, "Each group needs to create five goals. What are your five strategic goals for the year?" After the group spends an hour or so in teams, everybody should talk through their goals and agree—"This is what we need to do to align as a team." Then, each group should pick one person to read their goals to the gathering, and the other groups can ask questions about them. Also, assign a note taker during this phase to create a master list of the entire company's strategic-alignment goals.

To follow up on this goal setting, schedule a monthly meeting to review the goals with everybody. You can even do a Zoom call if everybody's spread out. Review the goals, then ask, "How are we doing toward these goals? Let's check in."

That last part is key: accountability. It's the leader's job to keep having one-on-ones with team members and regularly scheduled meetings with the team, both to keep their goals in front of them and to hold people accountable to actually do what they promised. What really works is that, once they've said it, and it's their idea, it's way easier to hold people accountable than if you said, "Here's what you need to do. Why aren't you a good team member?" They're probably thinking, *I'm not bought in, bro.*

Last, this team-alignment summit cannot be a one-time thing; it needs to be annual, because as you grow, growing pains are real. New team members come in, five years will go by, and all of a sudden you'll realize, *Oh, only half the team that's here has done this.* Just because *you* did it doesn't mean everybody did it.

As I've said, you have to do monthly reviews and accountability, but those rhythms are the lead-up to those two days. About six months before the summit, you have to invest with your leadership team to prepare for that meeting. All the leaders on your team, and you, should be shadowing all of your direct reports in the field, seeing them do their jobs. Watch them go about their job functions in pursuit of the goals you set at the first (or most recent) summit. The spending-time piece and the relationship-building piece, those are gradual, happening over time. Then, as you approach the time for the summit, the momentum almost reaches the mountaintop. After the summit, the regular rhythms and accountability at your company operate at a higher standard. The mountaintop has become your new baseline.

Every year, you raise the standard by realigning your team. That's how you have constant, never-ending improvement. This is why in my companies we call the two-day meeting the "Annual Team Alignment Summit." The expectation is built in; each year, this is what we do.

If you do this, it bats about 1,000%. The team will love

it because they actually crave it—they just don't know it yet. They don't have words for it. What the team has words for is, "People don't listen to me." What they mean is, "I don't think the leaders care about me." Because of misalignment nobody's talking to each other.

Speaking of sports metaphors, remember that when you win, the team gets the credit. When you lose, the leadership takes responsibility, just like all the great quarterbacks do. "I should have played better today." Or "It was a great team win." Or you can be like Cam Newton or other overrated quarterbacks and blame your team, and then your team will hate you.

Whether it is sports, business, or the rest of life, excellent organizations benefit from this kind of review, accountability, and clarity of communication. These improvements don't just occur in the business world; this is how human beings get better at everything. If you're the leader of a family, this all applies. If you're the leader of a church, this all applies. This is how you communicate strategy, build a unified vision, and empower your leaders. This is true organizational dynamics.

Once you've come to understand your core values; set clear, achievable goals; and aligned your team, you can turn your strategic attention outward to navigating the market.

4. Navigating the Market and Strategic Product Positioning

Recently, I put a 10-year vision presentation together for a company I serve as CSO. When you cast that kind of vision, you need to understand what is possible in the market. I do this when evaluating any company that I'm working with and when I'm coaching someone in a particular industry. Understanding the market is also tied to goal setting. People tend to base goals on random things like, "I did 10 last year, so why not do 11 this year?" Instead, what if the team looked at the entire market for a product or service as the ceiling for what is possible and then said, "Well, obviously somebody's out there paying X for this, why can't we increase our rates to Y, still 10% less than the highest price on the market?" Or "The entire market is producing $100 billion, why can't we do 1% of the market and be at $1 billion?" Or "I don't think there is a market comparison for what we are doing—the sky is the limit!" Then you set your goals. So, in a sense, market navigation feeds into and from the other four components of Executive Strategy as you iterate and grow—in this instance, navigating the market helps you refine and define your goals.

Because of this, when I take on a new company to help grow their value, I almost always start with macroeconomic data. I feel a fiduciary responsibility to myself, my family, my companies, my team members, and my friends who want to talk to me about economic trends to stay up to date with them. Just knowing what the size, potential, and capitalization of an industry might be helps you navigate it as a leader and as a team. Which industries are going up, which are going down? They very rarely all go down at the same time. **The market moves like an ocean. And if you just understand how money moves, then you can put yourself into the current and make a lot of money.**

Taking a past example: As Netflix's streaming service grew, DVD sales declined, and Blockbuster Video disappeared. If you can anticipate market movement, then you as a company, you as a leader, can make the right pivots to avoid becoming Blockbuster. When Tough Stump Technologies launched, it was an in-person drone (S-UAV) training company teaching military and first responders how to use a program called TAK, which stands for "Team Awareness Kit." Basically, it solves complex problems and teaches military special ops people how to program missions and to integrate technology and connect drones, trackers, and other assets to what they're doing on the ground.

When I started working with them as their CSO, one of their team members said, "You know, I created this online training program, but no one bought it. So, yeah, we just kind of shelved it." Then he went into the video files to show me the in-person trainings that he was working on. And I said, "Hold on, let me see this online training program you did." Because I had done a lot of market research in a prior life on how big, growing, and scalable the online learning market is. After he showed me the files for the learning management system (LMS) that he'd put together, I quickly thought, *This is it!* They were only charging $10 per student. Based on my prior knowledge of macroeconomic data in LMSs and online learning, I knew this was worth the extra time and investment to create a scalable product that the market would respond to favorably.

I estimated the market would be willing to accept a price point 10 times more than the current price, closer to $99 per student for a certification ... or $300-plus for a three-month enterprise license! Part of the calculation was knowing different product lines within market segments and what those markets were willing to pay, and knowing the difference between a subscription model versus a certification. We shifted the offering to be a certification—not just an online training that you pay $10 a month for, but a main featured product line called Tough Stump University, with the first course being the TAK Certification for a $300 user license. Users would have a three-month window to get certified for completing a course. The market potential for this product is exponential. I figured it could be worth $100 million by itself!

You might be reading this and saying, "Hey, that's cool, I'd like to be able to do what you just did, Dustin." To get there, you have to start with an attitude of curiosity. There are too many people walking around thinking they know everything, but I hope I never do. One of my goals is to die still feeling like, "Man, I had a lot more to learn."

This also feeds into the practice of listening that we mentioned in "Recruiting and Aligning the Executive Team," because you need to be a learner, and you must be coachable. A lot of this has to do with humility.

Your curiosity will drive your understanding of the market. Once you understand the market potential, then start looking at market examples and find a couple of avatars that you really like. Sometimes you can even draw inspiration from firms that are aren't competitors but are still parallel. If you're in the mushroom business, for example, you can look at other organic food or supplement companies and say, "Man, it's really cool what this other company that's not even a direct competitor of ours is doing." You can also look at the big-dog competitor, but it doesn't have to be the big dog.

For us at Totally Mushrooms (where I am an equity

partner and CSO), we found inspiration in Real Mushrooms, a Canadian company that is the top tier for quality but is actually relatively small; we're going to exceed their revenue this year. Their product is so incredibly good that all the health fanatics know Real Mushrooms is where to go for quality mushrooms, but they don't do any advertising. There's a reason they're so small; people have to find them, and our product has the test results to prove they're superior to Real's. We accomplished this by being humble and curious about what the best competitors in the market were doing. This is what healthy competition looks like: saying, "I really like what they're doing, and we need to emulate the thing they are doing so well. They're not cutting corners, and that's the standard we need to set for our team."

I had these claims validated by three other people. I asked people what the gold standard for quality was. They are not the biggest, but they are the ones that are not cutting any corners. An example of going to another adjacent company and taking best practices from them, as mentioned a couple of paragraphs up, is Athletic Greens. Athletic Greens is a great parallel example when you start to think about marketing. They have Joe Rogan promoting it. They're huge. Now, they are not a mushroom company, but they are a great company that we are learning something from, in addition to having better quality than Real Mushrooms!

To begin positioning your product, start by looking at the market as a whole, and then within the market, look at the frameworks of how your competition has built their business models—and then you start thinking about what you want to do. Ask questions like:

- What does my company consist of?
- What are my natural resources?
- What are we good at?
- Can we do all of it and vertically integrate, or should we stay niche and focus on what we are good at?

For example, Totally Mushrooms is vertically integrated. When you have a high barrier to entry and you can vertically integrate . . . you have a winning formula. Though difficult, it will let you dominate the market! I grew up in Dalton, Georgia, where most of the world's carpet is made in a town of around 60,000 people. The reason Dalton has remained the global leader in carpet production is the vertical integration of the entire carpet manufacturing industry is found in this small town. To duplicate it would cost more than what an investor could see receiving as an ROI in their lifetime.

Tough Stump, on the other hand, is a good example of company heads saying, "We solve a problem by doing a few things really well. Market demand favors us doing these few things. It matches our background and expertise. Vertical integration such as building our own drones doesn't fit our business model." As our CEO, Jarrett "Fish" Heavenston, says, "We aren't mining for gold, we sell the shovels."

With Tough Stump Technologies, we're in the government and first-responder drone-technology, geospatial-awareness, tracking, and training spaces. We picked a niche, and because we knew the market, we are thriving! Now, some of the things that we've changed within that niche are knowing segments of market demand (like an LMS versus in-person training) and how much better one will perform financially;

these are the types of pivots you can make with an understanding of your market.

- Step one, then, is looking at the macroeconomic data
  that defines the market.
- Step two is looking for exemplars, avatars, or parallels
  in other industries as well as the competition in your
  own. Find examples of people who make you want to
  do what they are doing, or who you can draw inspiration from, at least from segments of their business.
- Step three, you can combine inspiring segments into
  a machine that does lots of things well in combination. Integrate what you can, and fill the niches you
  can, but you must know your market.
- Step four, be humble. You will not increase your capacity if you are not curious and humble.

Humility is also required to keep up with the times. I don't
care if you got your MBA from Harvard—what do you know
about today's market? So many times I've been in board meetings and someone is quoting something that they learned while
getting their MBA, and I ask, "When did you go to school?"
And they answer, "1975." Most of the time, that means nothing to us today. If you don't know what's going on right now,
how can you lead anyone today? Unfortunately, this is happening everywhere, and especially in the C-suite, because they get
so much support from their executive team. Often they keep
so much data and relevant information from their team, they
don't actually have their finger on the pulse of the current business dynamics in the business they are leading. I mean, I've

been guilty of it. Once I realize I'm making decisions without taking that pulse, there is only one solution. I have to get out of the office, into the field, and work side by side with the team and listen to what they are saying, and what the customers are saying, until I understand the dynamics of the current market conditions. And that brings us to the final component of the First Strategic Pillar, Executive Strategy.

5. Adapting, Evolving, and Growing

Executive Strategy is your map and compass that guides you as a leader for every decision you make. It organizes your thoughts and decision-making processes into strategic departments that then helps you to know the answers to these questions:

> What should you be doing?
> What should you not be doing?
> Who should be doing what?
> When should they be doing it?
> How much should it cost?
> What is the timeline?
> What does success look like?
> How are you going to measure the activity to achieve success?

But none of these answers—or even these questions—are static. Nothing stays still for long unless it's dead, so you will need to adapt your values, goals, team, and approach to the market in real time.

The first time I tried to book my own hotel room when I wasn't the CEO of a big company, it occurred to me: *I haven't booked a hotel room in, like, 8 years, maybe 10 years.* And I double-paid because the buttons have gotten so much smarter. I hadn't done the "one-click buy" in so long either. I had wanted to see what the fees were going to be, but they were hidden. I clicked the button, thinking it was going to take me to another screen that gave me the summary to buy, but it had already charged my card! And then, in the small print, it said, "non-refundable." I'd put the wrong date in there as an example, so I immediately called to get my money back—but they wouldn't give me my money back. I was so frustrated, but I had to bite the bullet and book another room.

I left that experience feeling like, *Wow, you can become inept really fast if you aren't personally doing everything yourself*—which you can't. It made no sense that I would book my own hotel room when I was the CEO of 20 companies. You have a separate person whose job is to book your hotel room. But then, once that person is gone, you realize technology has changed. You must learn, adapt, and evolve.

Adapting and evolving means you're changing according to the things that you're observing. The implication is that things have changed. How do you prepare a company, an organization, to do something that involves that set of unknowns, to be that flexible, that adaptive? What plans can you design to prepare people for change? Any answer must consider that change management is difficult. Most people have a natural propensity to resist change. There are certain behavior profiles, like those who rate high for C (Conscientiousness) on the DiSC personality test, whose biggest fear is change. To instill a culture of flexibility change, it starts with the leader, and your team will do half of what you do right and twice what you do wrong.

Because your team will respond in this split fashion, you need to demonstrate to them your willingness to change and adapt, and then accept that your team will do about half of what you're willing to do. Some leaders are not willing to change, and many are not coachable—they're too stuck in their ways. Yet they wonder why the team doesn't change when they ask them to do things differently than before. It's like the apple doesn't fall far from the tree regarding a person's kids. If you're asking your kid to do something you're not willing to do, it's not going to happen—and in many ways, your team is the same.

> Your team will do half of what you do right and twice what you do wrong.

We've already planted some of the seeds for this section in the "Recruiting and Aligning the Executive Team" section, in terms of conducting monthly reviews and regularly returning to your vision, mission, and goals. Adapting and evolving requires you to act visibly; your team is actually watching to see if you do it. It's one thing to have an all-team meeting in person—most people don't even get to that step—but the best leaders in the world then schedule an executive meeting after the all-team meeting. They get together with Finance and the team that's managing everybody, and they review the notes and say, "All right, team, how are we going to do this?" They then begin making real changes.

Here are a few questions I often see that executives need to ask to adapt and change to grow their company:

- Do we need to change our pricing?
- Do we need to change our marketing strategy?
- Do we need to create or improve our business development processes, train the business development team to improve their skills, or give them better sales tools?
- Do we need to invest in new and improved technology?
- Do we need to overhaul our brand?
- Do we need to improve or create a customer service department?
- Do we need to diversify our product mix and invest in some new products?
- Do we need to improve, tweak, or redesign our compensation plans to be more motivational and help people focus on the work to produce the results we need?
- Do we need to review our manufacturing and vendor agreements? Are our vendors and manufacturers producing or providing the team's mission-critical resources in a timely fashion and in line with our contract?
- Is it time to vertically integrate?

Most leaders don't want to hear or do anything about the demands of change, because change is painful. Change takes effort and work. Change takes the humility to admit things can be better. Changes will always need to be made.

The question is, are you the type of leader who is willing to change? The answers to these questions are things that, honestly, most leaders just don't want to hear or do anything about, because the problems are not high level enough to really ruin the leader's day, but they're still enough to ruin one of your team member's days. Often the systemic problems in a company are rooted in a leader's weakness, and exposing that weakness and improving it makes the leader look ... well, weak. So again, it takes humility to admit your company has weaknesses, and that you're willing to put in the effort, do the work, and make the investment to adapt and grow the business.

To embody next-level leadership as part of your Executive Strategy, you must be humble. **Arrogance is most leaders' biggest problem, because what got them to being a leader is that they were successful.** They did some impressive things. They hit a home run, had a great idea. They're probably really smart and have a lot of things going for them. But if you really want to take your business to a supersonic, billion-dollar type of level, you need to embrace humility, or your odds of scaling it through other people are limited. Of course there could be exceptions, as with certain tech companies where someone can be a complete asshole, never have to deal with people, yet still hit it big. But if it's a person-based business (versus a one-person show), which a large percentage of all the other businesses outside of tech are, you

> **Change takes the humility to admit things can be better.**

need a leader who can listen, take feedback, and care, not just walk around saying, "This is my show—get on board or else." Maybe that worked in the dot-com era, but that's not the day and age we live in now. For the most part, **curiosity and humility are necessary if you want to scale.**

When you listen to your team give you any kind of real feedback, and then you immediately take action, it will make an impression! For example, when they tell you that a vendor is not supplying critical materials on time, you might call the manufacturer and tell them, "This is unacceptable." And then you can turn to your team and say, "We're going to hold them to the terms of their agreement, or we're going to find a new partner, or there's going to have to be consequences." The team will see that you're adapting. Or say in the next week, you get on the all-hands call after receiving feedback that the compensation plan is not motivating, and you say, "All right, gang, I heard you say you wanted a more motivational comp plan—here's your new compensation plan." Or, after receiving feedback that the company is lacking in customer service, in the team meeting, you say, "Hey, I want to introduce you to the new head of customer service. We just did a 30-day search. Her name's Veronica. Everybody, meet Veronica." That is when the team goes, "Okay, wow. Things really are changing for the better around here. We said this was a problem and look at how fast they solved it." **Because it does not matter what you say; all that matters is what you do.**

I have seen so many teams where the leader has taken the time to ask them, "What do we need to improve on?"—or worse, where the team has told the leader very clearly what they need to improve—and years go by and the leader does nothing. Then the team goes, "Oh, we've told them this is a problem. They're just not going to do anything about it." If you do everything we've already covered in the previous sections, but then don't execute, you'll never figure out how to implement team feedback. That might be worse than not taking the time to get their feedback and identify improvement areas in the first place. Don't ask people what they think you need to do to improve the company unless you are willing to adapt and change as they suggest.

Ultimately, if you really want to grow and build an executive strategy, you must be willing to change and adapt. It might take money and it might even cut into your personal pocketbook. If you're the owner of the company and you've got a 40% margin business, these changes might mean you've now got a company with a 30% margin business, and that means your income goes down by that 10 percentage points. **The best leaders are the ones who put the company first, over their own personal self-interest. This should be a guiding principle for every leader who wants to grow a company that has a real impact.**

If you're willing to reinvest into your company again and again, rather than trying to find every way to make another dollar just for yourself, you are modeling what a healthy company looks like. A healthy company generally has at least a 10% EBITDA margin that's growing toward 20% or more, but not at the cost of ignoring team feedback, or for the sake of making more money as the owner.

Philosophically, to stay focused on growth, you must align yourself to say, "I'm willing to make less money to make sure my team is aligned and willing to get on board to do all the things that I'm asking them to do to grow." Sometimes that means paying them more. Quite literally, you decide, "I'm going to pay myself less money, and I'm going to pay you more money." That will lead your team to grow the company. It can be that simple, and I've personally done that several times. Our salespeople were by far the highest-compensated sales team out of 30 related companies when I was creating a compensation plan for them. There were probably three or four different times in the history of that company where I lowered my own income to increase somebody else's, and then the whole company grew because of it. In my experience, it's worth it every single time. If you are willing to change, to adapt and evolve—even if it's painful—your team will be willing to follow you. And if you understand your core values, if you've set clear and achievable goals, if you've aligned the team and navigated the market with a posture of curiosity and humility, then that change will lead to growth, guaranteed. That is the difference an Executive Strategy makes: If you do the work, the results will follow. The question is: Are you willing to do it?

APPLYING EXECUTIVE STRATEGY TO YOUR WORLD

Now that you've explored the five components of Executive Strategy, the primary Strategic Pillar, it's time to apply what you've learned to your own context. Your world is not the same as mine, so you'll need to take some time, effort, and energy to translate it into something you can use.

A personal real-world example of applying Executive Strategy was when I had to create another layer of management. I had been promoted to CEO of the global family of companies and needed to create more capacity. I took two of our senior team leaders, made them "vice presidents of recruiting," and carved their extra salary out of my leadership compensation to help motivate them to recruit new team members. The plan worked well, and the two new leaders kept the recruiting momentum going and the business growing.

In the space below, describe an occasion when you had to decide how to increase your capacity as a leader by carving out something from your income to give yourself more time. It could be personally paying for an executive assistant, operations director, or marketing professional . . . or, as in my case, promoting someone to take an additional function off your plate and increase your capacity. Have you done this before? If not, use this space to list the areas of your business where you should be applying an Executive Strategy.

_____

_____

_____

_____

_____

_____

_____

_____

_____

Pillar 2

BUSINESS DEVELOPMENT STRATEGY: ACCELERATING GROWTH

The Second Strategic Pillar is your Business Development Strategy. **Business development is the lifeblood of a business. Sales is the fuel that propels your company forward.** Out of every 10 people I talk to who want me to help with their business, 9 say, "We have everything we need to be successful, we just need sales." I've literally heard entrepreneurs say, "That should be the easy part." If it was easy, then everyone would be doing it, and it wouldn't be a problem.

Most leaders' biggest problem is that they need help designing a selling system for the product or game-changing service they designed. Often the entrepreneur or CEO is also the salesperson and the rainmaker, and they're selling through pure passion and belief, but they've put no business development plan or system in place. It's just pure word of mouth, with the entrepreneur enthusiastically telling people about what they do, then praying that somebody signs up for it. Everyone else on the team is sitting around waiting for the phone to ring or for the entrepreneur to make it rain and bring in a big account for them to work on.

Aside from Executive Strategy, Business Development Strategy is the most significant need in the world of entrepreneurs. At the executive level, it involves identifying opportunities for growth, building strategic relationships, and developing and innovating on a business model. **At the heart of your business model is your sales model, and at the center of your sales model is your sales cycle.** If you want to scale, it is critical for you, the leader, to get your Business Development Strategy right. This is not something you want to delegate. It is the cornerstone of your growth plan's architecture. Your Business Development Strategy empowers you to create massive capacity to do more as a leader. It's how you move from being the top producer and rainmaker salesperson to being the executive who's running the business.

Business development is the art of identifying and seizing opportunities for sustainable growth. It involves strategic planning (or modeling), relationship building, and market expansion. All of this comes together in a very old, seemingly boring, totally misunderstood idea: the business model. If you take anything away from this chapter, make it this: **The model matters.**

If you get the model right, everything will be right. If the model is wrong, it does not matter how smart you are, how hard you work, or how great your team is. The business

will fail eventually, because you can't sell your way out of a bad model. Scaling a bad model only gets you more of something you don't want: losing. If you want to lose more time, money, and years off your life, keep trying to grow without a proven, sales-oriented business model. If you want to create more capacity—develop your business and scale it—then keep reading.

BUSINESS DEVELOPMENT STRATEGY OVERVIEW

What are the components of a Business Development Strategy? The strategy occupies a straight-line, big-picture, executive-level position and involves the following priorities:

- **Identify Growth Opportunities:** Regularly assess the market for expansion possibilities and opportunities.
- **Build Strategic Relationships:** Forge and nurture relationships that can open new doors. Always be selling. Always be recruiting.
- **Innovate in Business Models:** Stay open to evolving your business model to adapt to changes in market demand, technology, or the business environment.

These three priorities are necessary if you want to grow your business, and someone at a very high level in your company (in the C-suite) should always be walking through these steps. These may look familiar, because part of Executive Strategy (especially "Navigating the Market and Strategic Product Positioning") is geared toward setting up these

Business Development Strategies. These overarching strategies do actually work in the real world.

Let's apply these priorities to my time at the helm of a global conglomerate with over 3,000 business development team members:

- I spent a lot of time and energy **identifying and capitalizing on growth opportunities.** I was able to lead expansions into new markets and diversify the company's portfolio by recognizing and pursuing emerging trends.
- My team also understood the importance of **strategic relationships** in business development. The global conglomerate established key partnerships and alliances, which were instrumental in accessing new markets and resources.
- Most importantly, though, as the CEO of 20 companies, I was able to lead the conglomerate through a series of **business model changes and innovations**. By staying adaptable and responsive to market changes, the family of companies I served was able to sharpen its various competitive edges and, crucially, to grow in scale and profitability.

The executive-level business development innovation approach is not the only way to think about Business Development Strategy. Don't get me wrong; you need your executive-level team to be part of the Business Development Strategy, but in my experience, an even more foundational way to think about it is centered on your business model.

Your business model is built on your sales strategy, which encompasses your sales cycle. Your sales model and sales cycle are the lifeblood of your business, and they work on their own even outside of your executive team's management and oversight. If you can get your sales model and sales cycle right, and build everything else around them, then your company will grow without you personally having to be the biz-dev rep. Your company will scale without you having to make every decision, and you will win ... because your model is a winning formula. In other words, with the right sales model, you will increase your capacity and build a business bigger than you.

A lot of people in business haven't thought about their business model this way before now, and I get it. I literally have people try to make fun of me, saying, "Oh, I know, Dustin you're the model guy. Yeah, yeah ... ," and they try to diminish it. I just say, "Explain to me what about your business model is not important." And inevitably, they will say something really stupid, like, "We're just going to work hard." Good luck with that.

When you get the business model right, usually the business will grow. To share two examples from the real world, here's what it looks like to get the model, and therefore your Business Development Strategy, wrong, and then what it looks like when you get it right.

GETTING IT WRONG: THE PARTY IS OVER

When I became CEO of 30 different business units all at once, several of them were losing money. One was a party-planning company that had lost money for 17 years—but weirdly, its revenue was growing every single year, and the salespeople were making a ton of money. When I took over, it was doing approximately $20 million in revenue, but the model was not right. So while all the people in the business were making more money, the profits were declining. We finally had to all but shut the business down.

This company had 3,000 salespeople and almost 50 people on the operations side of the business. We wanted to fix the problems that were causing it to lose money every year, but the model was so messed up, and they had operated at such a deficit for so long, that trying to fix it was impossible. Here's the dirty little secret to these kinds of businesses: The worst thing you can do is to scale a business with a broken model, because all you'll do is make the problem bigger, and that's how people go bankrupt. The biggest risk you can take as an entrepreneur is diving in without clearly understanding your business model—risking everything, even your home equity line of credit, and leveraging yourself stupid for a great idea that lacks structure. Selling 10× more of a product than you did last year—when you lose money on each unit—is not scaling; it's suicide.

There are hundreds of ways of getting your model wrong: not having one in the first place, not innovating when the market is clearly shifting (say, away from physical video or DVD rentals toward digital streaming), scaling based on revenue rather than EBITDA profitability . . . the list goes on. You already know all this, though, because we see businesses fail all the time. Almost every time, there are significant problems with the model itself (like the WeWork example from chapter 1) in addition to problems of strategy, culture, and leadership. What I want you to focus on in this chapter are the elements of a business model that make it work. We are building on the components of the Executive Strategy we explored in the First Strategic Pillar and centering on the real dynamics of your sales cycle. What does it look like to get that right?

GETTING IT RIGHT: SCALING FROM LOCAL SEMINARS TO GLOBAL COACHING

The first company I ever built from scratch began as a seminar company. I got to learn how to work with a business partner out of the gate as an entrepreneur, and how to morph two proposed business models together. As we started with my new partner's plan, the seminar business, it was truly a creating-something-from-nothing business plan—just a piece of paper with our ideas on it. We were creating everything, the compensation plan, the marketing materials—we literally moved to California without knowing anything about how to run a motivational-sales seminar business.

We hired a consultant who gave us a VHS tape of a live, recorded "workshop," which became our sales process. We watched the tape to create our scripts, then we would set an appointment to go sell tickets to the seminar, and write the script of what we were going to say the night before. Then, a week before the first event, one of our team members said, "Hey, we just sold like 700 tickets at $300 a ticket, and we don't even know what we're going to say on stage at the big event! We should probably create our PowerPoints!" We were creating everything as we took the next step—building the plane as it was taking off.

I remember one manager had just bought 10 tickets for his whole team to go to this conference (by the way, I was probably 23 years old at the time). And he said, "Hey, I'm so excited to attend this conference. Who's the main stage speaker?" And without even hesitating, I said, "Well, I am." And he said, "Oh, okay." And I just shook his hand and walked out like it wasn't that big a deal. Those were the kind of wild and crazy experiences we had starting a company literally out of nothing.

But then we started to figure out an actual business model, and we pivoted into coaching, because people would attend our one-time event, and then they would say, "Wow, this is great, but what's next?" And we would say, lamely, "Well, you can come to the next seminar." We knew that our sales cycle, our strategy—our model—was not optimized. So, we changed it.

We didn't have another thing for them to attend, but we quickly figured out coaching was what people really needed to make a difference, to increase their production, and to improve their lives. I spent the next two years creating the coaching model, doing a lot of research, signing up for other coaching programs, figuring out how to sell ours, and learning how to create a coaching program. I made every mistake you can make, but finally, we figured it out. And very quickly, we discovered that coaching was so much more sustainable and scalable than seminars—it was a better model.

So, with 30 team members at the time, we pivoted the

entire business model. We'd been putting events on in three different cities, doing about $5 million in revenue a year, but we literally shut the entire seminar business down and went all-in on coaching. And it grew at 68% per year for over 10 years in a row, doing over $100 million in revenue in that time. It became "the thing." At the same time, I started a consulting company using what we had learned from the seminar business, and it scaled to over seven figures as well.

We coached over 20,000 people, one-on-one, and increased their income by over 40% on average. The parallel multimillion-dollar consulting business was also thriving. We were working with some of the biggest and most recognizable companies in the world. At one point, I personally had nine consulting projects going at one time, while managing a team of over 50 coaches globally. All of this stemmed from a strategic pivot—developing a new and improved business model by identifying growth opportunities and continuously iterating and innovating our sales cycle and strategy.

Managing that team and those processes, and putting everything together, all came from getting the model right. Get the model right and anything is possible.

BREAKDOWN: BUSINESS DEVELOPMENT STRATEGY

I have met thousands of CEOs, but I can count on one hand how many are "model-maker" CEOs who really understand business models at the highest level. Most people eventually figure it out through the school of hard knocks, even if they lack the language to explain how they created their business model, but the process tends to be very drawn out and painful. They don't even know to call it a "business model" or how to duplicate it. In other words, they won't be able to repeat their success.

They can't remember because their model wasn't strategic. They created a business model that could scale, but most CEOs only figure out how to do so slowly and with difficulty, and very few CEOs make a model in the beginning. My friend Matt Moore, an incredibly successful entrepreneur, says,

> Despite what most people think, running a successful business that produces several hundred thousand dollars in annual income is not the hardest part of the journey. In fact, the hardest part lies in two forms. First, in the commitment and follow through to start the business— as too many people talk without ever entering into "the grind." Earnestly, those who have quality ideas or product, coupled with determination and persistence, can reach a stage where their business can produce valuable income. But the second trap, and most difficult phase in my opinion, is scale. A large majority of entrepreneurs get stuck, harkening back to how hard it was to start the business, and become complacent when their enterprise hits its first, comfortable plateau that coincides with their *mode de vie*. I advise them to drop the comfort and press on. The best entrepreneurs are constantly tearing down and rebuilding their business model—scaling the growth into new phases without fear—as failure is not an option.

The Model Matters

The way that you can create capacity and scale your business bigger than you as a leader, as an entrepreneur, is through a well-designed and thought-through business model, one that you can prove works again and again. When you have such a model, you can almost turn your brain off regarding many of the things that consume CEOs and rob them of sleep. I can name 10 CEOs right now who are thinking about things every day that should be automated, that should just be part of a business model, but they insist on doing manually. They're taking up space in their brains because they haven't created a structure to automate the important parts of the business. It's like re-creating the wheel every single day. What the model allows you to do is not even to have to think about it, because you have everything defined from the outset.

With a winning model, you reduce everything to a metric and turn your business plan into a formula for success. It contains a schedule on which each metric should be achieved. Knowing what the input and output will be guides everything. Typically, when starting out, you personally will create the model for running the business. Besides being the creator, you're the salesperson, operator, admin, and bottle washer all in that same day. Over time, however, you need to ask yourself, *What am I doing today that I could hire someone to do for less than what my time is worth?* To know what your time is worth, divide how much you made last year—or even better, how much you plan on earning this year—by 220 (the typical number of workdays in a year). Then divide that number by 8 (the typical number of real hours you are working and producing in a day), and that should be how much you are paying yourself per hour as an entrepreneur, and that should be your cutoff for hiring someone to perform tasks that earn you less than this hourly figure.

For example: You are paying yourself $150,000 per year. That's $681.81 per day, $85.22 per hour. Any task you are doing that you could hire someone to do for less than your hourly rate is literally wasting company resources and money. Don't waste $85.22 on something that should only cost $25.

As your business grows, the best way to invest any profits is in people who can operate the systems you've created to run your business and free up your capacity to focus on higher-level growth opportunities. This process never ends. The best leaders are the ones who lead by example, do a job, create a model, recruit other people, and teach them how to work the system they created.

This is something that comes intuitively to me. I don't know how I learned this. Even when I was selling books door to door, in order to figure out how to break the company record, I created a strategy—a selling model—where I had certain systems I would perform during nine specific timed points and intervals throughout the day, six days a week. Then I had a system for every hour on Sunday. Selling door to door was a microcosm for modeling an individual selling system. I found the same principles could apply to building and scaling a global coaching and consulting business, international insurance businesses, a drone tech business, mushroom tech farming and distribution company, and medical

AI software business . . . and to virtually every other type of business out there. The key to all of it is a working model. But what makes a model work?

The Twin Engines of Your Sales Model

Your Business Development Strategy is a step-by-step process that walks you through the first engine of your sales model: a sales cycle. What is your sales cycle? Most people have never created one before. They've never thought of it as a process for generating business. When you think of it as a cycle, you can start to create a framework. In addition to the sales cycle, the second engine of a Business Development Strategy is creating a team-building and recruiting system. You need to have a never-ending recruiting system with metrics that drive expectations, a compensation structure, and a commission plan to pay people (your sales team). To do business development at the level the company needs to grow, you need dialed-in leadership and an accountability structure to ensure the Business Development Strategy is being executed properly. This is how you create a system of exponential growth.

After creating your concept or viable initial product and determining your price point in the market, creating a compensation plan is often the next step in building out a Business Development Model. **A radical idea that I often share with other CEOs, some of whom have a lot of resistance to this idea, is to create a compensation plan for themselves that fits within a scalable business model.** This freaks entrepreneurs out because they're used to paying themselves all the money. To think of paying themselves less is crazy to them—they will say, "I've got bills to pay. You don't understand. I can't afford to pay myself less money." If that's your approach, you will be a company of one. You'll be the CEO of yourself, forever. Until you're willing to share the pie, you won't be able to scale a business. Take a close look at your revenue and your cost to produce goods. Once you have your cost of goods, then you can also look at your cost of sale and build in a margin of what you're willing to invest to have you or somebody else sell your product.

I once received a brilliant piece of advice from a wise mentor of mine. Spencer Hays, who passed away very wealthy, was the founder of a large custom clothing company named Tom James and built several other successful companies. He was the majority shareholder of the large global conglomerate where I became CEO after he passed away. He donated something in the neighborhood of $300 million worth of his art to the Musée d'Orsay in France, for which President François Hollande awarded him and his wife the Legion of Honour—an occasion I witnessed at the Élysée Palace in Paris.

One day over lunch, Hays said, "You know a great way to build a business model? Start with your EBITDA profit margin and set a financial goal for your company. Your minimum profit goal should be 10%, but you might have a profit goal of 15%, 20%, 30%, and whatever you want that EBITDA profit margin to be—start with that and then build the model backwards. It's so simple, and yet nobody does it."

So, if you start off with 10% at the beginning, and you want to show a 10% profit at the end of the year, you figure out, "Okay, how much does it cost for me to make my product?" And let's say that 50% of your revenue goes to producing your product. So now you have 40% left. Well, you could carve out 20% for your cost of selling, and then you have 20% for admin, corporate overhead, and your salary. What's unique about you as an entrepreneur is that, if you're a rainmaker, technically you've reserved the ability to pay yourself 40% when you're first starting out, because you're also the admin *and* the salesperson.

Then what you could do is to say that within that 20% for selling, you could pay all of it to a salesperson that comes in and works on straight commission. Or you could do a 5% override for a sales manager, because it's going to take a lot of work to manage your salespeople, and you offer a 15% sales commission. If you make yourself the sales leader, then you get paid 5% of every dollar whether you sell it or they sell it. You can also have your ordinary compensation plan as CEO or president or founder or whatever title you give yourself. You also get to sweep the profits (after reserves) at the end of the year if you choose to do that with your business model. The point is to do the work of thinking through a sales model so that you can figure out how to pay people to sell your product.

The Business Development Team

Next, you think, *Who are the right people to sell my product?* Then you start considering what a sales team would look like for you. There are all kinds of different sales teams out there: outside salespeople calling on folks, setting appointments, meeting with them, and selling products and services; inside salespeople on the phone either answering inbound leads or calling out to sell; online salespeople sending emails and selling through online messaging; door-to-door salespeople; and people selling in retail stores.

With so many different types of salespeople you could hire, start figuring out the right type by creating an avatar for your customer so you have an idea of who you are selling to. You have a product, you have a service, but the first thing you should think about when creating a Business Development Strategy is: *Who's going to buy this?* Ask questions about who they are:

- What's their demographic?
- Is it men? Women? Both?
- Where are they located?
- Is there an age range that's applicable to your product or your service?
- Do they have certain ideologies? Are they Republicans? Are they Democrats? Are they Christians? Are they atheists?
- What do these people want or need?
- Do they care about healthy living?
- Do they want to make more money?
- Do they want to save time?
- Do they want a better lifestyle?
- Do they want to travel more?
- Do they want to be more productive?
- Do they want more fulfillment, satisfaction, and joy?

The more you can refine the avatar of your ideal client, the more it will help you think of what your ideal salesperson might look like. Then you can create an avatar and profile of that salesperson for your product or service that matches the avatar of the customer. You do not want a salesperson who has never played a sport in their life selling to customers who buy sports equipment.

Now you can write a job description that will attract the type of salesperson that you want to hire. Don't just literally describe your product or your company—that's boring and stale. Instead, craft it to attract and motivate the person that you're trying to recruit to click on your ad and submit a resume, saying, "Wow, this job sounds like it's built for me!" Then when they tell you that, you can laugh and say, "I actually *did* write it just for you, because you are the perfect salesperson for us, the one that I was trying to find."

In addition to writing a good job description, choose carefully where to post it. If you're selling skateboards, advertise somewhere where skateboarders would be, somewhere like a Reddit skating community or the website of a skateboarding magazine. You could sponsor a skateboarding event or talk to people at skate parks. Your ideal skateboard sales force probably isn't on LinkedIn or at a career fair in their interview suit.

If you're trying to find someone to sell insurance for you, LinkedIn is a great place to be, or similar professional services. If you're trying to hire a recruiter, LinkedIn has millions of recruiters that are active there every single day. Making sure you place your job description in an optimal location is like fishing. If you want to catch a tuna, you should probably go to Cabo, Mexico, and fish in the ocean, as opposed to going to a pond on a golf course and expecting to catch a tuna. Recruiting is exactly the same way. Are you even fishing in the right water to attract the person that you're trying to attract?

To summarize our high-level mental process for a sales team or Business Development team-building strategy:

1. Decide how you will pay your salespeople. Create a sales compensation plan.
2. What kind of people do you want? Create a sales rep avatar.
3. How do you attract those people and find those people? Create a job description and role definition.
4. Set clear expectations and find the winners. Create a recruiting and interview process.
5. Know how you're going to manage your team. Create a sales management system.

I rarely find leaders that have a dialed-in interview process for recruiting. Most people just talk to someone and if they like them, they say, "You're hired." The problem with that is people need to feel like they've earned it. It's kind of like having kids. If you don't make your kids do chores to get money, and you just give them money every time they ask, then they will lose the stuff that you buy them. They'll take for granted how special it is that their parents give them toys for Christmas, for instance. But if you make them earn their money for chores, they'll spend their money on more of the things they want, and they'll treat them much differently. Team building is exactly the same way. If you have a consistent recruiting process that makes people jump through hoops, they'll feel like they've earned it, and they will value it.

As an example of such a recruiting process, first, have candidates submit a resume as usual. Apply a review process to screen out unqualified resumes based on a set of requirements and standards (e.g., college degree, CPA, experience with QuickBooks or Excel, sales experience).

Second, email strong candidates and say, "Hey, thanks for submitting your resume. Here's my website. Check it out and reply and let me know why you want to work here." And then you wait. Let them jump through the hoop that you put in front of them. Chances are if you get 50 applications and respond to 20 of them, 10 or 15 will actually do this exercise. A step like this saves you a massive amount of time in screening all 50 candidates—it's basically a self-screening trick.

Third, have a well-defined and "dialed-in" first interview. I like listening to their story for about half the call and then telling them the company story for nearly the next half, before finishing by having them talk about their vision. How does the company's vision align with their own? (I usually try to not talk about money on the first call.)

Fourth, give them two assignments on the second call. Say, "Hey, I'm going to email you some more information about the company. I'd love for you to tell me in writing why this job appeals to you," and give them some kind of second assignment in addition to that—for example, have them go to your website and send you a summary of what they like about what your company does. Then at some point, usually the next call, you walk through how the money works for them—in other words, how they get paid. Walk them through some details of the job requirements, then ask more direct questions to ascertain if they really have what it takes to do this job. You can also have them interview with another team member to discuss the ups and downs of the job, company culture, and so forth.

Fifth, I like to have them see the job. Have them come watch you or somebody else do the work, then walk them through the offer and the details of their compensation package, and the expectations of the position. *Your* job is to emotionally prepare them for the challenges of *their* job. If anything, make those challenges sound harder than they really are. Setting very clear expectations during the interview process is one of the most important things you can do, yet so few people do this. Establishing expectations after you've hired someone tees them up for failure. But doing so during the interview process, especially for the hard parts of the job, with no sugar coating, ensures they will sign up with full knowledge of what sucks about the position. They're literally saying, "I understand how hard this is going to be, and I still want to do it." Otherwise, if they feel like you sold them on joining your team, but then find the job is different or much harder, you'll have a disgruntled employee from day one. So, you might as well go ahead and tell them how difficult things can be. Later, when things get difficult as you'd described, they'll think, *This is exactly what that hiring manager told me.* They won't get disgruntled and quit, and you'll gain credibility as a leader.

Sixth, onboard them. Somebody's first day on the job is

the most important workday they'll ever have—yet again, so many leaders miss this. They hire a team member, give them a desk and a phone, and maybe (rarely) order them business cards. The new hire is left to wander around like a lost puppy, hoping somebody gives them direction on what to do. Maybe the leader meets with them for an hour that first day and takes them to lunch, but it's more getting to know the employee and "How's everything going?" with no structure to it. "Figure it out" seems to be most companies' default onboarding process. Instead, you should plot an hour-by-hour, day-by-day schedule for the first 90 days. Every hour should be scheduled for a new hire, so they know who they're with, what they're doing, and what they're learning.

Personally, I like creating weekly onboarding themes.

- The first week's theme is "company knowledge" or "company history," or "industry knowledge" or "product knowledge."
- The second week is "technical," such as how to work with the computer systems or CRM software, how to sell, or how to call on someone.
- The third week is "in-person learning"—shadowing and watching people do the job.
- The fourth week is "mentorship," where they're watching someone and someone else is watching them.
- The fifth week is "taking the training wheels off"— they're trying to do the job on their own, but they are checking in frequently.

One big caveat: Every job is completely different, and not every onboarding process is going to look the same. The point is you need to have at least a detailed, written, 90-day onboarding system for all new hires.

Even though I just gave you a very generic outline, it will be better than 90% of what other people are doing out there. The key for your sales team, whatever their onboarding process may look like, is to walk people through your sales cycle. All those other things are important, but now that you know you have the right human, and they've been onboarded, you're going to really teach them how to do the thing that you need them to do—sell!

The Selling Cycle

Most often, the cycle of the sale starts with a question: How do you generate leads?

Step 1: Lead Generation

There are dozens of ways to generate leads. You can create online selling funnels in which people click and fill out forms to submit a lead. You can buy a list; you can literally use SIC (Standard Industrial Classification) codes and get a list of people in a certain demographic, in a certain industry that you're trying to sell to, with their name, phone number, and email address. Or you can generate leads through the number one method: referrals. Referrals are God's gift for working your business the right way, and cold-calling is God's punishment for not asking for referrals.

To elaborate: It boggles my mind how so many people

don't ask for referrals. Often the reason they don't do it is fear of rejection. You do need a process for asking for, expecting, and getting referrals. It usually involves not using the word "referral," but instead jogging people's memories, painting the picture of the type of person you're looking for, doing the thinking for them, and creating a cheat sheet of people who you know would be helped by what you are offering them.

Again, you can also knock on doors, have a retail shop, farm an existing book of business for a cross-selling opportunity, find secondary connections on LinkedIn—even cold-call if you must. There are so many ways you could generate leads; those are just a few.

Next, you need to have a process for the second part of your sales cycle: knowing how to set an appointment.

Step 2. Appointment Setting

In an interview that I did with Matt Moore, serial entrepreneur and best-selling author, on my *All Things New Ventures* podcast, he tells a story of his mentor, who went to a conference in the 1970s. He paid $50 or so for his conference ticket and flew to Houston. He sat in the audience, then a guy walked onto the stage, where there was a chair and a table with a phone on it. And then he said, "If you want to be successful at selling and business development, there are two things that you need to know. Number one, you need to pick up the phone and call somebody. Number two, you need to get off your butt and go see them."

And the guy walks up to the phone, acts like he's dialing, does a role-play of what the phone call would sound like, sets an appointment, hangs up the phone, and then says,

"Now I'm going to go see him." And he walks out the door, supposedly to go see the person he called, and off the stage, leaving everybody sitting in this conference room. And he never comes back. Everybody's sitting there staring at each other, and they were all pissed, because they all paid money for that. Matt's mentor flew to Houston to go to the seminar, and the guy was literally on stage for less than three minutes. And that was the entire seminar.

Now, Matt's mentor told him, "What's crazy is I've attended dozens and dozens of sales seminars, read dozens and dozens of business development and sales books, and hands down, by far the most impactful training I've ever been to was that training." **Pick up the phone, set an appointment with somebody, and then go see them.** And that is Matt's secret. Matt is a wildly successful entrepreneur, and that's what he does. That's it—nothing else. It's crazy. He's very successful, and he just picks up the phone and calls somebody, sets an appointment with them, then he goes and sees them wherever they are. That's what everybody needs to do. All you need is a process for how to call people and a script for what are you going to say.

In the book *Crucial Conversations*, written by five PhDs, they say that scripting is the highest form of communication.[3] So many people think scripts are beneath them, saying, "Oh, no, I don't need a script. I'm good. I have a way with words. I know what to say." The reality is, a script is simply proven words that work. If you have proven words that work, why would you say anything different? Wouldn't it be stupid to wing it if you know exactly what to say to get an appointment 90% of the time?

So, if I have words that are proven to work, and I know 90% of the time, if I say these words, 90% of people are going to meet with me, wouldn't it be ridiculous for me

> **Scripting is the highest form of communication.**

to say something different? Yet that's what most salespeople do. Most entrepreneurs do it, too, because they don't want to sound "canned," " corny," or "cheesy." Well, congratulations. In your effort to not sound "corny," you're getting about a 10% closing rate, and your business is not scaling. And you wonder why? Or you can actually write down a script that causes somebody to go, "Yeah, I'll meet with you," and then train not only yourself but also other people how to say those words.

Usually when it comes to scripting, less is more. Being assumptive is the way to go, and all you're trying to do in that second step of your sales cycle is get the appointment. You are not trying to sell your product or service. There are some businesses where it's transactional; the prospect already has filled out a form saying, "I'm interested." That's different; these might be a one-call close. In most businesses, however, this is rare. If that's not your business model, then usually **the goal of the first call is setting the appointment.**

Step 3. The Presentation

This is where you're meeting with the person to uncover their needs and wants, and to provide a solution to their problems or needs. Again, have an actual written-down script, framework, or process—whatever you want to call it to make yourself feel good. Now you are creating a selling process that can scale.

If you don't like the word "script," so be it. Call it a "written-down selling strategy" for when you walk in the door, or get on the video call, and meet with somebody.

For example:

- What questions are you going to ask them to build rapport?
- How are you going to uncover the need that they have for your product or service?
- Once they say, "Yeah, you know what, I do need your product or service," what are you going to do to create pain and agitate that need to the point where they want to change?

Why create pain? Because **pain causes change, and the best salespeople in the world are the best at asking questions, listening, and unearthing pain through asking questions, then providing a solution to that pain. That's what selling is. That is the highest technical level of selling.** With that being said, there is an even higher level of selling.

The essence of selling, and **what makes somebody a truly great salesperson, is the ability to transfer belief and energy to other people about what you do.** That's how simple selling can be. That is why most entrepreneurs are successful. That's why most entrepreneurs are able to sell even if they've never technically been trained as salespeople. The reason they succeed despite the lack of training is because they have that belief in what they do. They have energy and enthusiasm and passion, and they can transfer those traits to other people. As soon as somebody else has the same belief that you have about the thing you do, that's when they buy.

Step 4. The Close

The next step of the sales cycle is some type of closing process. If you're there in person meeting with people, you'll offer to compose a quote or a proposal of some kind. Then, after ending the initial meeting and getting all the information you need, you'll schedule another meeting to give them the quote, presentation, or proposal. Delivering this successfully is a whole process with its own script, leading to the close. **Closing is an art. You need to have three to five closing techniques memorized that you can pull out at any time to close the deal.** Here are some of my favorite closes:

- **The Self-Closing Technique:** *"Why is this something you want to move forward with today?"*
- **Choice of Two Positives:** *"Which option do you want move forward with, one or two?"*
- **The Jedi Mind Trick:** *"If I'm reading you right, it seems like you think this is a good idea, right?"*
- **NLP (Neuro-Linguistic Programming) Assumptive Choice of Two Positives:** *"Let's go ahead and get you started. All I need to know to get you set up is your email. Do you use a personal or work email address?"*

The best closes are done before the presentation. It's where you answer all the objections up front, do a trial close, and get an agreement before you present that "if they like what you're about to show them, then they will give you a 'yes' or a 'no' today." Think of your closing process as a series of traffic lights:

- **Green Light:** The prospect is with you and proceeds to filling out the paperwork.
- **Yellow Light:** The prospect has questions or concerns. Answer the objections through telling third-party stories of other customers who had the same concerns but moved forward anyway.
- **Red Light:** The prospect is not a fit. Get referrals and move on to the next prospect.

Step 5. Collecting Money

Next, there's usually a step where you collect payment, and that is a process in itself.

A lot of people wonder why they have huge accounts-receivable issues. The reason is that they don't have a well-defined Business Development process with a system for collecting money. Streamlining cash collection, receiving it on the spot, enabling digital payments, having a QR code—you need some way to make it easy. If you make it hard for people to give you money, your business will suffer, but if you make it super easy, it's like Amazon. One of the reasons Amazon is the biggest company in the world is the

> The best closes are done before the presentation.

single-click purchase. I love listening to the Lex Friedman interview with Amazon CEO Jeff Bezos, who said 1-Click was a game changer that took them to the next level. A lot of people forget that Amazon invented that. Why is that so important? They made it easy to collect cash. Everybody in the world can emulate their Business Development process. Take a page out of Jeff Bezos's book and do it for your business. If it is hard for somebody to give you money, you are going to have a very limited customer base.

As a personal example of how poor money-collection practices can cost a sale: My wife and I were planning a trip to Bali. However, we couldn't get the first hotel, the one we really wanted to stay at, to accept any of three different credit cards. No one would respond to our inquiry, and we couldn't get anyone to pick up the phone when we called. They said, "Call us during our business hours," when Bali's business hours are past midnight in America. They made it very difficult. After the third email and attempt to book with them, we just found an Airbnb, which took our money immediately. We said, "Screw the cool hotel we wanted to stay at. We're going to stay at this Airbnb," because it was easier to pay.

So, whatever you're selling, make it easy for people to give you money. Then, after the life of the sales cycle completes itself and they've paid you, and you've done a great job with your service, then you get referrals.

Step 6. Referrals

Referrals should always be a step in the sales cycle, because they propel it like a wheel. The referrals lead to the next person, to the next step, and it never ends. When you do this right, you might have to spend the first six months of your business cold-calling, buying leads, going to trade shows, and so forth. But once you're up and running, and you have a decent amount of customers, if you're really good at asking for referrals and getting multiple referrals from each person, then you'll never run out of business.

The Jet Fuel: Compensation

Building out your business development team can't be emphasized enough. So many entrepreneurs focus on the idea, the product, marketing, raising capital, and they get all the pieces and parts, but they neglect the actual selling machine that's going to propel them into the future. Your sales engine is the most important part of the business. It's so crazy seeing companies out there that are well funded and have a great idea but no concept of how to sell the thing that they've created. If you're reading this and realizing that this is a weakness of yours, immediately pursue making it a strength, because if your biggest strength is your business development strategy, then your business will flourish and grow.

It's not as fundamental as Executive Strategy, but if you get the Business Development Strategy model right, you can sell and recruit your way out of nearly any problem. You may not be able to legal, or finance, or market your way out of most problems, but you can sell and recruit your way out of them. The thing is, to get the sales engine really humming, you must have a compensation plan that's working, and your sales team needs to be making a ton of money. This is the best thing that could possibly happen. **Ensuring your**

salespeople are the highest-paid people in the entire company is a very good thing.

The kind of logic that some people use for compensation is so bizarre to me. I have to coach CEOs and founders on this all the time, because they say, "Well, the salespeople can't make that much money," and they have an actual problem with somebody who's out there growing their company—making it rain—earning so much. They complain, "They're the highest-paid person in the company, and they might not have the longest tenure," or, "These other people have been with the company for five years. How can I justify paying this business development person twice as much as everybody else who has been here longer? We need a compensation plan that goes down as the sales go up, so people don't make too much money." And the answer should be simple. But it's not for all companies. Salespeople are growing your company, and they're on straight commission or something like it. They take on more risk, which should bring more rewards. The exception to this is if you have a plan or people who want a large guaranteed salary in order to do their sales job; then, offering them a smaller, limited, more moderate commission plan is recommended. More risk = more reward.

Whatever your sales team's compensation plan is—base plus commission, straight commission, or some kind of

> If you get the Business Development Strategy model right, you can sell and recruit your way out of nearly any problem.

bonus structure—if you get that plan right and you protect your margins, then every time they incrementally sell more, the company makes more. Under this practice, when your salespeople are the highest-paid people in the entire company, you know the company is growing. I've seen people come in from trying to salvage a messy situation, and the first thing they do is see these people making all this money on the sales team, and say, "Let's cut commissions." And that's the death blow of a company. If you're trying to turn a company around, cutting commissions is usually the last thing you want to do.

Now, I say that with a caveat, because I personally have been involved in situations where the commission structure was the problem that was sinking the company. And in that case, when the commission structure is structured such that the company never makes money, and will go out of business if you don't change it, you do have to address it. That's different than most situations where there is a lack of Executive Strategy and there are all kinds of problems everywhere you look. Just because commissions are an easy place to target, because salespeople are making good money, doesn't mean that it's the right place to start changing things if you're trying to turn a company around.

If you get the model right, and the compensation plan is part of that model, then just let it go. Don't fix something that's not broken. I was talking the other day to someone at a growing company where a CEO was coming in and meddling—specifically, with the well-established compensation plan. People were getting demotivated and had stopped working, and revenue was declining—and they wonder why? It's very simple to me. In the military, they say, "Don't mess with pay and chow."

When somebody's going into battle for you, you don't tell them, "Hey, I'm gonna pay you less for this battle." In the middle of a war, you pay your army whatever you have to pay them to win. Cutting compensation will demotivate people and wreck your revenue quickly.

Recently, I got into an argument with a buddy who's very successful but has the philosophy that paying salespeople too much is wrong for the company. He thinks it's not being a good steward. He said, "Well, your margins would be so much better if you paid the salespeople less." And I say, "I would much rather have more revenue." Less margin, but a healthy margin, with a revenue that keeps going up forever. He's had a company where the revenue has stayed the same for eight years, but he kept making the margins better. Now, he did make a bunch of money selling the company, but nobody else there did. My philosophy leads to sharing in the growth, making sure the company has a healthy margin, but you need to grow the pie. Then it doesn't matter how you slice it up—it's a bigger pie.

This is why I like business models that have exponential growth potential. To be clear: I'm not dogging the people who have a smaller, healthy, margin-based business, because that's better than 99% of the people out there. I think it's much more exciting seeing something that can go from $100 million to $1 billion, and just keep going, so you can recruit people who are excited about growing that type of company, something with unlimited potential. In any case, don't be afraid of paying people good money.

Here are some examples of how to design commission plans:

Straight Commission

Start with figuring out what the business can afford from a Cost of Sale perspective. Again, take your EBITDA margin, subtract your Cost of Goods, subtract your General Admin, and see what you have left. Next, figure out what it takes to hire the kind of sales/biz-dev people you need to sell your products or services. Some companies have a very basic sales process and it's more like hiring "order takers" where the commission plan can be lower. Other companies have very sophisticated sales cycles that take a high level of skill and require a much more generous commission plan. **The work should equal the reward.** Often you see plans with 10%–30% commission rates. You also can add components and features to your commission plans to compensate many people for doing specific income-producing activities.

For example, you can have a 5% referral fee for anyone who refers a paying customer. Then you can have a 10% sales commission for the biz-dev rep who walks the client through the entire sales process. You can have a 2% sales-leader override compensation plan for sales leadership, as well as a 3% bonus structure to be used for sales incentives. In this example you'd budget a 20% Cost of Sale, but you'd pay it out to the people doing the specific income-producing activities that your commission plan helps motivate.

Base + Commission

Sometimes longer sales cycles require a starting base salary to get a new biz-dev rep up and running. For example, in some insurance businesses getting a book of business established to the point of sustaining a full-time compensation plan often can take six months or longer. In such cases, it makes sense to create a lower base salary plus commissions. Often a time horizon can be attached to the plan to allow the onboarding process to be established and the new rep to become self-sustaining. However, I always recommend creating a date for a compensation plan review upon hiring a new rep where base salaries and commission plans can be adjusted according to achieving certain metrics and results.

For example, the salary might be $30,000 plus a 2% commission for the first six months to a year. Then you can review their activity and results by backtesting their sales or forecasted sales pipeline and applying the full commission plan to the forecast to see when they should be making more money on straight commission versus remaining on base plus a small commission. Let's say that the normal commission plan is 20% and the average sale price is $10,000, for $2,000 commission per sale. A biz-dev rep will need to sell two customers per month and will now make more money on straight commission versus a $30K base plus 2% commission. (A general rule with a plan like this is once someone goes straight full commission, they cannot go back to salary plus a small commission.)

Base Salary + Bonus

Typically this type of plan entails a quota to justify the base salary. The comical element of base plus bonus plans is usually they are simply a straight commission plan camou-flaged as a guaranteed base salary. This usually means the quota is based on a percentage of sales and calculated from the size of the rep's salary, and if the rep doesn't hit their quota, they will be fired. So what might seem to be a safer option for biz-dev reps in actuality becomes more risky, because companies cannot have people on payroll on whom they're losing money.

For example: The base salary is $80,000 plus a $20,000 bonus if they hit their annual quota. Using the same assumptions as the base + commission above example, they would need to sell 50 clients in the year as their quota to earn their bonus. They would also have a stipulation that if they have several months or quarters in a row of selling under three clients per month, they will be terminated.

Measure What Matters

When it comes to selling systems and business development systems, you need to measure what matters. There's a book about this called *Measure What Matters: How Google, Bono, and the Gates Foundation Rock the World with OKRs* by John Doerr, who created the idea of Objectives and Key Results (OKRs) and Key Performance Indicators (KPIs). He was a key consultant for Google, U2, and several other world-famous organizations. The thing he instituted for all of them was to reverse-engineer their goals down to daily activities, put them into a tracking system, and have them track them every single day. He created dashboards where they had to review their activity every week as a team and create an accountability structure to ensure everyone committed to the activities needed to get to the end goal—in short, an income-producing activity-tracking system.

If you focus on tracking your income-generating activities, things you must do on a daily basis, then the results will come.

For business development, OKRs/KPIs typically look something like the following:

- How many phone calls do you have to make per day?
- How many decision makers do you need to talk to per day?
- How many appointments do you need to set per day?
- How many presentations do you need to run per week?
- How many proposals do you need to send out per week?
- How many customers do you need to have per month?
- How much revenue do you need per quarter?
- How much profit do you need per year?

Start with the clear, SMART goals that you articulated in chapter 1 for your Executive Strategy. Then, reverse-engineer these goals down into daily activity. When I was figuring out how to sell books door to door as a college student, the key metric was 30 demos a day. If you worked 80 hours a week, did 30 demos a day, had 20 sit-downs a day (and I had around a 50% closing rate, so I knew I'd have 10 customers a day), then you would meet your goals. The average is something like 2 purchases out of 30 demos, which the company I worked for had been doing for 150 years. They know they can train thousands of salespeople, give them a script, and say, "Show the books to 30 people a day, 2 people are going to buy, and you're going to make this much money in a summer." You can figure out metrics like this with every business. Part of the challenge of knowing how to do it, and then actually doing it, is that it takes discipline from the leader.

In fact, it takes discipline from everybody to really pull this off, and that's why most people don't do it; they'd rather shoot from the hip, then offer a lot of excuses for why they don't track things. "Oh, that's not our culture. You know, we don't want to be Big Brother." They give you a bunch of bullshit that really comes down to laziness, because the real questions are whether or not you want to grow and whether or not you believe in accountability. If your culture is unaccountable, it's chaotic. Whatever people say about why they can't measure what matters, it actually comes down to the fact that they're not willing to. Maybe, as the leader, you might need to care more about growing the company than about people liking you and thinking you're "cool." **Often it is unpopular to hold people accountable, but it doesn't mean it's not the right thing to do. Everyone needs accountability.**

Maybe you need to step up your vision and your passion as a leader and ask yourself if you really want to do this thing. Or are you just jerking around? Because if the leader really wants to grow, if the leader really believes in what they're doing, then everyone else will follow; this is a top-down leadership requirement. The only way I've seen this accomplished is the leader, the CEO, or the founder must buy in and drive it, or it will not work. This cannot be delegated to a lower-level person. Everybody is watching the CEO, and if the CEO isn't tracking anything, then they don't track anything.

Let's say you've never measured what matters, but you have an existing business. If you really want to get tactical, get your top producers to be your case study. Before you roll it out to all of your salespeople, have your top 2 (if you're a small company), top 5 (if you're a medium company), or top 10 (if you're a large company) create your "scorecard." Get together in a meeting and ask, "What are the things that are our critical KPIs?" Every business is different. For instance, your scorecard could include leads generated, how many appointments are set with leads, presentations given, numbers of quotes given or prices discussed, how many closing processes are started, whether objections are answered, and (always) how many times salespeople ask for referrals. These are the things that you track.

Some companies have different industry-specific things that they want to track—there are plenty. You and your top producers must figure out what those are. Then you tell your top producers, "Hey, for the next week or two, we need your help. You're going to take a piece of paper. I don't care if it's scrap paper or a spreadsheet. You can be as organized or as cowboy as you want. All I care about is that you track your activity." Then you have everybody sit around a table and write down your KPIs—calls, reaches, appointments, set presentations, closes—and then you put Monday, Tuesday,

Wednesday, Thursday, and Friday across it and draw lines like a grid. Then you make tally marks for each activity on each day. That's what I used to do. That's the most effective one for me. There's something about it that makes me use it, versus the nice, pretty, printed kind. I like the dirty, messy cowboy scorecard with etched-in tally marks for my wins.

Then, put all the scorecards up on a wall or the screen to display for everyone to see.

The format of the scorecard depends on what your job is. When you're going door to door, tape it to the back of your notebook when you're physically out there. This way, when you get in your car, you flip over your notebook and put a tally mark for what you did at that door. If you're sitting in front of a phone, then it's sitting right next to the phone and you're doing tally marks at every single phone call. People can also use digital scorecards if you want to get fancy. Salesforce has integrated this now, so there are CRMs that will do this, but the point is that you must do it. No company gets a pass on this.

If you want to be successful, and you want to be a badass Business Development company, then you have to track what matters and you have to report it. You need to hold people accountable. I like creating leaderboards. **Take the top three in every category and publish or display them publicly.** Once a month, say, show the whole team. I don't care if you've got 100 people, 1,000 people, or 5 people, you say, "Hey, congratulations. Here's our leader for these categories." And sometimes just the recognition is enough. If you want to and you have money, then give them a gift card.

Incentive Plans

On that gift card point: We used to spend something like $100,000 a year on giving prizes away. Salespeople are highly motivated by incentives and recognition. People will work harder to get a Starbucks gift card presented to them in front of their peers than they will for their own paycheck. Harness this instinct by creating a leaderboard and have it focus on income-producing activity, not just production. When you give prizes based on activity, you drive growth. That way you're not giving the same top producer the same prize every month. These are incentive plans, and they are an extension of your compensation structure. **People will run through walls just to get the recognition, but the way you do the recognition matters, so publicly recognizing the activity as much (if not more than) the results is key to building out an incentive plan.** Of course, first you'll need an incentive plan—most people don't have one.

Once you establish the incentive plan, the next level, if you can swing it as a lot of companies do, is to create an "incentive trip." The reason people don't do incentive trips is they think they can't afford it, but they are highly motivational. Back when we were a $1 million business, we still did a trip—just a cheaper one. We created a Mac Daddy Level, which was something like, "Hey, if you produce $500,000 in revenue"—something like half the company revenue—"we'll pay for you and someone else to go on the trip. If you hit $400,000, then we'll pay for you to go on the trip and give you a couple hundred bucks if you want to take somebody. If you hit $300,000, then we'll pay for you to go on the trip. If you hit $200,000, we'll pay half of your ticket, but you pay the other half. And if you hit $100,000, you're allowed to go, but you have to pay. If you're under $100,000, you can't go on the trip." That was our first incentive plan—and again, we were a $1 million company.

Usually, you should plan for about 30% of your salespeople to qualify for the trip, and then you reverse-engineer a budget. I have always budgeted 1% of revenue toward incentive trips. If you are a million-dollar company, then you have $10,000 to dedicate to a trip. Five people probably can go on a really nice trip for $10,000. And there you go—you have an incentive trip. Five people are going to go somewhere, maybe a local destination that you have everyone drive to . . . but you have $2,000 a person and you have an incentive trip, and you're a $1 million company!

The trip is not the only incentive, but it's the big one. You also should have monthly incentives: if you sell X amount per month, you get some level of incentive. We used to have a book where people would get points every month and you could choose your prizes, and there were big-screen TVs, Xboxes . . . we even had a clear kayak as a prize in the incentive book! Part of it is finding cool stuff that people wouldn't spend their own money on. The psychology behind a sales incentive plan is fascinating. People look at the incentives, then they work so hard, making more money than they've ever made, and they could just go buy a $500 kayak, but, man, they'll produce $30,000 in a month to *win* that $500 kayak and love it. It's incredibly motivational. Remember, if you are a smaller business, the incentive could literally be $10 gift cards. You launch a contest to win a $10 Starbucks card and people will go nuts to win it.

———————

We've explored the sales cycle, sales strategy, recruiting, training, the actual mechanics of the sale itself, compensation plans, business development, selling systems, measuring what matters, metrics, KPIs, and incentive plans. This is your sales model, the machine at the heart of your business model. There's another level of Business Development that we've hinted at, but that you, as the leader, need to consider in more detail, because only you can do it: Executive Business Development.

Executive Business Development

As I mentioned at the beginning of this chapter, while most of this Strategic Pillar focuses on building out your team to grow your business, there are high-level elements to Business Development Strategy that only the CEO, the president, the leader of the company can do. A leader should be spending their time doing the things that only they can do. This also overlaps with the necessity of delegation. **You should spend 90% of your own time during the workday on things that only you can do.** If somebody else out there can do whatever it is you're doing, then find that person as fast as possible, hire them, and delegate those things to them, because the odds are that the functions with the highest pay value per hour are typically those that only the CEO can do. Then, **if you're**

an entrepreneur in the early stages of growth, the game that you play is that you're constantly backfilling yourself—meaning, hiring people to do the work you are doing with lower pay values per hour as the company makes more money. If you are doing the work that an executive assistant could do, then you are earning the same amount as an executive assistant for the task you are doing during that time.

As you grow and have more money, you can go from doing everything yourself to hiring more people to get more work done. That is the number one thing you can do to grow. Dave Ramsey has been a mentor of mine for many years—we typically meet annually—and he always says, "The best investment you can make is into your own business." You will get an exponential return from investing in more staffing and creating more systems to add greater capacity to your day. Again, this is by far the best investment you can make as a leader.

That said, at a certain point, there are certain Business Development opportunities that only the top leader can do: strategic partnerships, mergers and acquisitions, joint ventures, national accounts, and other significant opportunities. Often what this entails is one CEO calling another, which has a different dynamic. A lot of times, a CEO calls the head of a similarly sized company and asks to chat for a few minutes, and the other CEO will take the call because they figure, "Well, you know, this person's busy, too, so, yeah,

> **"The best investment you can make is into your own business."**

I'll hear what they have to say." Even if it's a vice president or a Business Development person, trying to get an appointment with that CEO can often be very challenging.

You see, if it's a peer-to-peer selling opportunity, then the CEO inherently has to be the one to sell to the peer at another company if it involves a significant business development opportunity. This is not always the case, but sometimes it is the best way to get into important doors.

For example, no major trade in the NBA will ever happen without the GMs talking to each other. They are not delegating that kind of deal. Mergers and acquisitions are likewise tricky. I've seen leaders try to lean on their second-tier leaders, like getting their VP level to go find opportunities and negotiate to acquire a company. It doesn't work. It gets weird. They will accidentally say a bunch of stuff that the company can't commit to. They find they don't really know what the exact fit you're looking for even is. It tends to waste a bunch of people's time.

Top-level leaders typically only need to attend high-level meetings featuring activities like these:

- Structuring deals
- Negotiating contracts
- Settling equity swaps in acquisitions or mergers
- Meeting with outside investors
- Discovering the debt of a prospective company
- Building relationships with bankers and structuring financial tools
- Understanding how they are basing their company valuation

In 99.99% of companies, only a very small handful of people know that level of information—usually the CEO, treasurer, CFO, maybe the head of Ops or one other executive. There's likely also a small finance team that really knows the financial dynamics of the company. For you to negotiate at a high level, assemble strategic partnerships to acquire companies, sell off parts of companies, expand to different states or countries, or expand from being a one-shop business to multiple locations, you need the CEO or other top leader to figure it out.

Expanding from one country to another has especially complex dynamics at play. Legal obviously will be involved at this level of executive business development. For example, I tried to use our US in-house legal team to do business in Estonia, London, Lithuania, and Bulgaria, and it was like speaking a different language (pun intended). I had to personally go, interview, and hire lawyers in London and Estonia. No other person besides a leader could have done those business development activities.

Along with the high-level biz dev that top-level leaders can do, I personally think **it's cool for the leader to have an actual sales goal and to publicly say, "I'm going to personally kick in X amount of revenue this year."** Setting revenue generation goals is healthy for leaders because you're experiencing all the same emotions that your sales team does. This commitment will put pressure on you, but I think it's a healthy pressure.

There are growth opportunities only you as the leader can identify, strategic relationships that only you can form.

It is your job to continue to pursue a healthy, innovative business model.

APPLYING BUSINESS DEVELOPMENT STRATEGY TO YOUR WORLD

When I became chief strategy officer at Totally Mushrooms, I understood the scale of what could be done in one of the fastest-growing food and supplement industries in the world. The first thing I did after assessing the current business development model was completely change it. Over the previous three years they had sold one Totally Mushrooms modular grow farm. There was no sales process, no sales team, no marketing strategy or team, and they were out of money, having produced only about $100,000 the year before I joined the team.

I went to work, personally figuring out what a pricing structure should look like, crafting a sales team compensation plan, establishing an investor model to pay back the customers, and recruiting and training a sales team. Then, with my wife's help, I sold the first several customers to create a path for others to follow.

The result of creating a Business Development Strategy for Totally Mushrooms was that the business development team sold over $4 million in grow farms in less than six months! Operations even told us to stop selling so they could catch up to Sales. That is the best problem any business can have.

When was the last time you personally went into the field to sell your products or services? Do you believe in the philosophy that you cannot teach what you do not know, and you cannot lead where you will not go? If not, why not? Most people are simply afraid of rejection or failure, and they try to hire people to do the hardest part of any job . . . selling. The reality is if you want to grow your company and achieve maximum capacity to grow staff bigger than yourself and a few other people, you need to get into the trenches and sell first. How can you make this happen? When are you going to pick up the phone and schedule several appointments to sell something? I promise you will get a renewed sense of belief and confidence when you set a personal sales goal and achieve it!

Set down the book right now. Pick up your phone and call your top three prospects. Schedule appointments with them for sometime in the next two weeks. Go meet with them and sell them something! Use the space below to capture any notes or takeaways from the experience.

_____

_____

_____

_____

_____

_____

_____

_____

_____

Pillar 3

MARKETING STRATEGY: CREATING A SELF-PROPELLING MARKETING MACHINE

A solid Marketing Strategy will help you go from being an entrepreneur to becoming a CEO with the capacity to take the business to the highest possible level. This third Strategic Pillar, Marketing Strategy, is an expression and extension of the core identity of your company and the work you did in the first Pillar, Executive Strategy. The bridge from Executive Strategy to Marketing Strategy partly comprises the values, team, and goals that you developed as part of your Executive Strategy: your marketing team, marketing goals, and brand identity. Once you establish those three components of your Marketing Strategy, then you can reach the world with your brand by understanding your target audience, creating effective marketing campaigns, and using data and technology to build and nurture long-lasting customer relationships. At the center of it all is one thing: your brand.

MARKETING STRATEGY OVERVIEW: WHAT IS MARKETING?

Marketing Strategy is a broad topic, like the other Strategic Pillars, but it's not perceived as such. People naturally tend to think about legal, finance, or business development as having plenty of moving parts and responsibilities. But with marketing, they imagine it's this one, single thing that you do. I've talked to leaders who say things like, "Yeah, we have a marketing guy, he does our website." I follow up with, "Awesome, what else does he do?" The look on their faces is comical.

Imagine hiring someone to run an entire university sports program but they only know how to play tennis. They can't structure everything around tennis; there will be blind spots and problems down the road. It's the same with hiring a web developer or graphic designer and relying on them for your entire marketing strategy. You're the executive; it's your job to have an overarching vision for your brand, or to find someone who can build a team of marketing specialists to help you establish your brand identity, get that brand out into the world, generate leads, and help increase your capacity and grow the value of your business.

Here are two examples of how to get a Marketing Strategy wrong, and one example of how to get a Marketing Strategy right.

GETTING IT WRONG: META AND MORE

When I heard Facebook had changed its name to Meta, I thought, "That's the craziest, most ballsy thing I've ever heard of." Their stock went down dramatically right after, and at least in the short-to-medium term, some analysts estimated it cost them $500 billion.

Even with all of that, no one today calls it "Meta."

I wonder if Mark Zuckerberg would do it all over again, given how much brand recognition Facebook already had.

Facebook made what it perceived as a strategic move because it was trying to set itself up for pivots: "Hey, we're not just Facebook, we're also Instagram. We do so much more." It could work out in the long run, but in my opinion, it was too hard, too fast. The market wasn't ready. It's a great example of what not to do: Don't overspend your brand equity. If you are going to make a change like that, it's best to try to do so in the early stages, when no one knows who you are. Otherwise, if your company is more established, try to slowly and strategically introduce the market to your new name and brand over time.

Think carefully about what changing your company name will cost you. At the consulting company I founded, a situation early on forced us to answer this question. The original name was actually "Success Starts Now!" and to be honest, I didn't love that brand from the very beginning. I had a business partner who's a great guy, one of the best salesmen in the world, yet he was committed to calling the company "Success Starts Now!" with an exclamation point at the end.

I just couldn't get behind it. It felt cheesy every time I

said it. I found myself making fun of it as I was saying it, and I had to change it so I could have integrity in being part of the company. To everyone's credit, we did change the brand name and identity, but it was a process. We had to get the whole team together to deliberate. We made a list of names. We hired a marketing company to help us do the research, and we landed on "Southwestern Consulting." From there, we developed a logo to establish our identity, following the whole process for logo creation: color scheme, font, and a moniker and tagline that accurately represent you.

In the end, it's about counting the cost. "Meta" might be around for a long time, but I think even they would tell you that it cost them way more than they expected. For our consulting company, it was the right time, the rebrand was worth it, and after that series of decisions, the firm took off. When it comes to your business, especially your brand identity, it is always worth spending the time it takes to get it right—the earlier the better.

GETTING IT RIGHT: BLUE RIBBON SPORTS (WHO?)

A great example of the right way to do it is Nike. When Nike first started, their company name was Blue Ribbon Sports. They went with that name for years, but it just wasn't connecting with people, and they felt it didn't speak to who they were.

They had decided to start making their own running shoes after ending their relationship with a Japanese shoe manufacturer. After a number of failed attempts, the founder,

Phil Knight, was up against a deadline for naming the shoe. He received one last suggestion from Jeff Johnson, the company's first employee. Johnson said the name had come to him in a dream the night before: "Nike," the winged Greek goddess of victory, who was associated with athletics. The name was short and had a strong sound because of the "K" near the end.

With only moments to make his decision, Knight agreed with Johnson, and Nike was born. A few years later, with the success of the shoe line, they changed the whole company name and brand to Nike. It's interesting that you can change a company's name without changing its legal structure, because the latter is very expensive and involves a lot of behind-the-scenes paperwork. For this reason, Nike was still legally "Blue Ribbon Sports" but doing business as "Nike." In any case, Nike made several right brand moves: a short, punchy name; the "swoosh" logo they developed shortly after; the black, white, and red that became associated with Nike over time. It all just clicked.

Ultimately, it's about doing the work, investing the time, looking at all your options, and then making creative decisions that you can live with. Then your creative team or contractors can go execute.

BREAKDOWN: MARKETING STRATEGY

Marketing is a broad category of skills. When people say they are in "marketing," it is like saying, "I play sports." Not every Marketing Strategy is needed for every company. It is important to understand the gamut of Marketing Strategies that could be deployed to help increase your capacity.

Marketing strategy can include the following:

- Building your marketing team
- Building a strong brand identity
- Understanding your target audience
- Creating effective marketing campaigns
- Embracing marketing technologies and integration
- Mastering social media marketing
- Nurturing customer relationships through marketing

Building Your Marketing Team

First you need to identify your biggest needs. Marketing is such a broad department that you can make a lot of mistakes after hiring the wrong type of marketer for what your company needs. Follow these three steps before allocating time and resources to hiring your marketing team:

1. What are the biggest marketing needs our company has over the next 3–12 months? Marketing-need categories include updated branding, new website, revised sales collateral materials, lead generation, media and PR, marketing emails, CRM automation, and marketing funnels for follow-up sequences, to name a few.

2. Create a marketing-department vision for your company. How many marketing positions do you need now? How many will you need as you grow? What

would a rough budget look like for this department? What are the marketing team's KPIs? What is the return on investment (ROI) for creating this department?

3. Start small and grow. Create a job description and pay range for the most urgent need you have. This will vary for every company. Some companies need to start day one with a CMO to tackle a huge undertaking out of the gates, some need just a graphic designer, some need a website design team. Start with the biggest need and grow from there.

One person that I hired as my marketing manager was hesitant to wear the "PR officer" hat. They were a graphic designer by training and didn't know how to do PR. Many times, and I'm the most guilty of this, we hire someone and expect them to do the job of 20 people, but the best people do figure it out and become leaders of their department. For example, that marketing manager took on the needed extra work outside of her job description and ended up getting promoted to vice president of marketing. Over time, as you grow, they let you know they need more help.

It's normal, as you grow your business, to start by hiring generalists. If you don't have the money to hire a PR person, a graphic designer, a web person, and a brand manager, then find someone who has some general skills in most of these areas. Make sure to set proper expectations. The key for every leader when building out any department is to clearly communicate that you understand you're asking them to do work that might one day require 10 people.

Early on, if you're a start-up, acknowledge you're a start-up. Don't try to hide it, don't be ashamed of it, and don't sugarcoat it. When you're interviewing a marketing person, tell them, "We're a start-up. This year we did under a million dollars, but we have big goals, we have a big vision. We're going to be doing $10 million within the next five years and then beyond." Communicate that you see marketing as an important arena and you're willing to staff that department as it continues to grow. If the new hire is capable of wearing many hats and figuring out all the company's different needs, one day they might have the opportunity to lead their department.

When you interview somebody that way, it's motivational. The right person will see it as an opportunity. You're also setting yourself up for future success. You're giving them permission to realize, when budget season arrives, they can ask for somebody to help as the company continues to grow.

Through this method, you'll eventually build some form of marketing team. Most start-ups will have a small in-house marketing team and will hire specialists ad hoc. Take public relations. Unless you're a huge business or you work in a field that's in the public eye, you don't need a full-time PR person, but it is nice to have one on retainer or contract. You'll know how much they charge you per hour, and they'll already be familiar with your company; they know you. At that point, you can just contact them to put out a fire or announce something exciting, and they're ready to go. Legal services, like for intellectual property, are another example. Outsource what tasks your company needs depending on the frequency.

Some businesses don't need a full-time graphic designer or email outreach manager, while others would benefit from a full-time database expert on staff. It's about meeting your day-to-day needs. For marketing, some companies decide to outsource most of the apparatus, then hire a marketing company or create a marketing department, depending on how their needs evolve.

Two Marketing Strategy Points to Consider

Ultimately, the key metric that I hold marketers accountable to is lead generation. Leads typically are why we are developing a Marketing Strategy. Brand recognition has value, but if you're doing your job right, people should be calling you and saying, "I'm interested in what you're doing" because of the branding. The marketing is so strong that they want to talk to somebody about it.

Also, it's important to keep marketing from becoming a silo, and to avoid the "us versus them" mentality, which is unfortunately very common in businesses. Marketing needs to be integrated with sales, ops, and every other part of your business. I don't know why this stigma is out there, but your marketing staff are an important part of the entire operation. The mission, vision, and values that we explored in your Executive

> **The key metric that I hold marketers accountable to is lead generation.**

Strategy translate in your Marketing Strategy to the brand identity, messaging, and then the individual marketing projects taking place under that umbrella: website, collateral, one-sheets, press kit, PR database, email, social, case studies. Obviously someone needs to make all that stuff. That's why it's critical to build a marketing team that's integrated into the rest of the company, because they will translate your core strategic beliefs, your identity, into both your brand and every message that goes out into the world to communicate that brand.

Building a Strong Brand Identity

Over the past 20 years of starting and leading businesses, I've realized a large part of the value I bring to companies has been the process of creating a marketing or brand strategy. I've helped create many company brands, logos, and identities; re-brand established businesses; produce marketing collateral pieces ranging from websites and sales brochures to business cards; craft marketing email sequences, lead generation funnels, and video commercials and testimonials; write lots of marketing copy; develop and host podcasts . . . and more. Your brand identity must be interwoven into everything you do. It's not just a logo or a website, it's what determines your Marketing Strategy at the highest level. This was something I learned organically, as most entrepreneurs do, through the school of hard knocks. Plenty of entrepreneurs at some point

> Marketing needs to be integrated with sales, ops, and every other part of your business.

are also the start-up's marketing person (unless they have a business partner, spouse, or somebody else who's just naturally good at marketing-related things), especially if they're a creative visionary.

Entrepreneurs can also be creatives, which is the category I fit in: "Visionary Creative Entrepreneur." My creative outlet was nerding out over the visual elements of our brand identity—choosing the color scheme, creating the logo, and establishing the overall design. When I became CEO at a global conglomerate of 20 companies, one of the first things I did was to personally lead the global rebrand process. I found a top-recommended and award-winning branding and marketing firm out of Chicago and hired them. I ended up personally creating the concept of the logo, even though we paid a company a million dollars to do the design work. Everything they sent us seemed not to connect the dots and wasn't really what we were trying to do with our new vision. I tried to let them do their job, but finally I said, "Look, the T needs to break through the bottom. The N needs to break through the top. It needs to be slanted forward. The font needs to look rugged and gritty." Ta-da—the new logo and brand identity were born!

In the end, it was really a collaboration and brainstorming process. I personally gave them the specific direction they needed, they did exactly what I said, and then we had our logo! I executed the same process prior to that at the consulting and coaching company I cofounded and led, then proceeded to do so again with my current company, All Things New Ventures. The point is that, as a leader, having your fingerprints on your brand identity is paramount, especially if you are a creative visionary entrepreneur. Your company's brand identity is an extension of you as the leader.

Now, I didn't actually design the logo. I didn't turn on my computer and learn Adobe, but I visualized and conceptualized it, then shared my vision of the concept with professional marketing designers who knew how to take a concept to reality and make it look cool. That's where I think the intersection of executive leadership and working with specialists overlaps. When you are talking about your brand and your brand identity, you are in the world of marketing, and everything in that world is affected by your brand identity. Think of branding as the roof over the marketing building. If you want your marketing to be effective, focus on getting the branding right first.

> Your company's brand identity is an extension of you as the leader.

Most people don't realize when they see a brand how much thought has gone into its creation. Sure, you can make something up quickly and then get lucky, but most of the brands that people trust have been very intentional—they have experienced marketing professionals helping them to think through what the brand identity looks like. Once you go through a process of ensuring the name, logo, color scheme, and fonts are right, what you need produced from that is typically a brand guideline book—something most companies don't have.

Let's say you're going to change your website. You should

be able to physically hand the developers the schematics of your brand, which they can use to create the site exactly in line with your vision. If you don't have a brand guideline book, the best marketing companies will create one for you for a fee.

Part of understanding your brand identity is understanding who you are. Usually, these companies do interesting exercises to get a better grasp on that. They'll ask you questions like the following to home in on your brand:

- "What three existing brands represent you the most?"
- "What movies do you think your company is most like?"
- "If your company was a car, what kind of car would it be?"
- "Looking at the color wheel and thinking of the emotions each color evokes, which colors represent the emotions your company wants others to feel?"
- "If your company was an animal, what would it be?"

Recently, I had a phone call with one of my equity-partner companies about acquiring a product line and merging it into our Totally Mushrooms brand. It's a perfect example of how a master brand can help structure business deals. You have to think through whether this is a simply a merger, an acquisition, or both. Are we keeping the brands separate? Are we rolling the product into our lines, rebranding it under the master brand, or are we cobranding?

Companies like Procter & Gamble and Johnson &

Johnson have acquired massive numbers of brands that they've rolled into one superstructure brand. Those brand guidelines help them to functionally grow their business through mergers and acquisitions. Then there are other companies like Google, which has Google Earth and Google Phone. Google is a good example of a hybrid style, where most of their purchases take on the name "Google" for the master brand, but sometimes retain their brand, like You-Tube. This is where marketing and branding intersect with strategy. If you have the Marketing Strategy right, then the business will be right. Your Marketing Strategy is upstream of everything else you do in the realm of marketing.

Understanding Your Target Audience

If you go back to the "Business Development Team" section in chapter 2 ("Business Development Strategy"), you'll remember that we explored your customer avatar (or the people you are selling your product to) on the way to finding your perfect salesperson or sales team. Because this is one of the places where Business Development Strategy and Marketing Strategy meet, I'm not going to repeat the work we've already done here. Go back to that section, your notes on it, and your exercises, and you'll see that you already know your target audience, because you had to articulate that in the process of building your sales team and business model. You should have an accurate picture of your customers' demographics and tendencies, and where to find them.

Creating Effective Marketing Campaigns

Marketing Strategy is first about establishing your brand with a powerful name, logo, and brand identity, then building your marketing team, and then understanding your audience. The priority that quickly comes to the forefront, however, is working on the messaging you are sending out to your audience and the media that you are using to do that.

A key part of marketing involves creating compelling copy: the written and spoken messages you are sending out to the world that communicate who you are and what you do. What are people seeing about you online, in print advertisements, and in commercials? Whether it's on your website, social media, commercials, or billboards, ensuring that the words are communicating a unified message about who you are and what you do is paramount. Many times with marketing, you're distilling the essence of who you are as a brand down to a simple message your audience can easily understand. Doing this is often not easy.

That's when you can start creating marketing tools like a website, which will build off your branding and messaging. The words on your website describe what you do, your branding reflects who you are, and the site puts both out into the world. Along with the website, your marketing collateral represents your brand and describes what you do. Marketing collateral includes things like a selling brochure, a one-sheet summary flyer, a promo video, and a sales landing page with a QR code.

In addition to business development, marketing collateral

can also be used for team building. You can give recruiting packets—a folder containing company information that explains who you are and what you do—to candidates during interviews. Press kits can be sent to media agencies to generate stories, and press releases can be written for your first branding announcement, major rebrands, key executive hires, big announcements, and so forth. Press kits often bleed into public relations, and a lot of times PR comes under the marketing umbrella, which can sometimes confuse people. PR often is viewed as reactive—cleaning up messes and fixing issues in the media—but it also can be a proactive tool for helping the market and growing the company when managed appropriately. PR professionals can get you news interviews, podcast bookings, magazine features, even product placements in movies and TV shows. All these PR tools are next-level marketing strategies.

There are also the traditional marketing options such as billboards, commercials, and search engine optimization. One of my former executive coaching clients is a billboard guy, but he also got search engine optimized when the internet was first becoming popular back in the late '90s. He built a website and got all the keywords for Nashville real estate. It doesn't matter if he's technically the best realtor in the world, because he got his marketing system down, and that's why he's consistently the number one agent in the state of Tennessee. He knows if he spends $10 million on billboards, he'll make $50 million in real estate. It's the same principle as clicks and keywords. It's simply math; it's churn and it's scale. It also helps him recruit. He doesn't have to be the best recruiter in the world, either, because he can call any realtor in the world and say, "Hey, I can give you a hundred leads a month, do you want to come work with me?" That's what the other agents don't have.

Once you have your team, brand, target audience, and message, you can figure out which media works best for getting your message out. Most of the time, that requires data— lots of data.

The Data Age: Utilizing Data and Analytics in Marketing

The movie *The Social Dilemma* did a great job of freaking people out about the dangers of data-driven marketing. While big tech companies are possibly infringing on people's privacy, it doesn't mean you shouldn't develop a data-driven decision-making marketing strategy. Targeted digital marketing works for a lot of companies, and most of the time it's worth it. If you understand your customers' demographics and where to find them, and you have your KPIs established, you can pay for keywords and have a decent understanding of what the ROI should be for your investment.

I had a client in the mental health space who'd crafted a precise formula with all his keywords dialed in. If you typed in one of those words, he knew you were in a bad place. Our consulting and coaching business created his sales process and selling scripts, and his closing ratio went through the roof. This guy was extremely smart, and he could see exactly how much he could pay for each click in relation to his revenue. The company would spend millions every month on these keywords and make tens of millions as a result. We were training his sales team on what to say with the leads, but he was the front end on bringing those leads in. As a result, his company was able to help a lot of people, because he knew the words to pay for.

There are businesses out there where it's worth figuring out that game, and it's a lucrative game to play. But the trick is understanding what the keywords are for whatever it is you're doing and selling. Consultants can optimize your website and your lead funnel to capture leads and send them to you every day. You'll pay a dollar, ten, or a hundred a click, but you need a process to convert that into real earnings. The question is, can you break it down to a math equation like my mental health client did? This obviously dovetails with the chapter 2 sections "The Model Matters" and "Measure What Matters."

There are a lot of options for digital marketing, but you can calibrate what you're doing by reading books or accessing other resources, or by handing off those tasks to your marketing people. The point is to cast a wide net when considering the most effective tools, then test those tools using actual data, real numbers. The math will tell the story here. Again, this is integrated into the Business Development Strategy and sales engine that drives your company's growth.

Embracing Marketing Technologies and Integration

Another area where marketing intersects with other departments is in developing learning management systems (LMSs) and building out customer relationship management systems (CRMs). This is where your executive team, business development team, marketing team, technology team, finance team, even your legal team come together. You're building out your client relationship management "brain," whether it's Salesforce, HubSpot, Monday.com, Infusionsoft, or anything in between; that is the brain of the company. Your CRM contains your database, so database management often falls under marketing, but it's really a beast in and of itself. Often the heads of marketing and IT will partner to lead the process of creating a CRM or LMS. Regardless, these types of projects are too important to fully delegate, and as the leader of the company, you need to be intimately involved in creating your CRM or LMS. I've seen investments into these sorts of large, expensive systems managed incorrectly and take down a small, growing company.

What do CRMs include? If you're making sales calls, you should be updating the CRM system after every call, every day. Here are a few of the types of information you'd want your CRM to manage:

- Have all new leads been entered and assigned an owner?
- When did a salesperson call the lead?
- What did the client say on the call?
- What was the next step from the call?

After meeting the client in person for a presentation, document what transpired by entering notes from the meeting:

- What did they buy?
- How much did they spend?
- What's the next step with them once they are a client?
- When are they renewing?
- Have you had any other customer service interactions?

Your CRM also needs to tie into finance and legal. Streamlining payment processing, calculating commission, collecting and storing contracts, and setting up auto-payments can take your company's operational systems to the next level when implemented correctly in a CRM. Don't have multiple different systems that can't talk to one another; the goal is to have them all interconnected in one or two smoothly operating systems. Consider the following example sequence:

- Your IT, marketing, sales, finance, and legal systems can all intersect from something as simple as a lead coming in from your website. Potential clients go to your website and fill out a form saying they're interested, and that automatically goes into the CRM. Your marketing team can set up automated emails, triggered by these leads, that go to the sales team.
- The salesperson calls the clients, then updates the contact card to reflect whether the person is interested.
- If so, after selling the prospect they can send the client a DocuSign contract that is stored on the CRM.
- The client's credit card is also charged through the CRM, which is then reported back to finance so payroll can pay out commissions, notify operations of a new customer, and so forth.
- Then it goes all the way back to marketing: The client is flagged within the CRM, which sends a welcome email that says something like, "Congratulations on buying our product. Here's three tips that you need to know about what we do and how to take advantage of what you just bought."

- You can have the client opt into your monthly news-letter, where they're constantly finding out about new offers and new products.

This is all inside the CRM, where every function inter-sects. Marketing is typically still the quarterback that drives the decision to create a CRM. It is usually worth your per-sonal time and attention to ensure your business's CRM is set up properly and attempt to automate as many of your company functions as possible. Is it difficult, expensive, and time consuming? Yes—but it's 100% worth it! CRM develop-ment is also a function where marketing intersects heavily with your executive team. If you have a CMO and a CTO or a CIO, have them work together along with the rest of the executive team on designing the CRM.

Because Marketing Strategy overlaps with Business De-velopment Strategy in several areas, you need people to talk to one another to close sales after they enter the marketing funnel you have created. Such funnels can take a customer all the way to the finish line. For some products, the mar-keting funnels can take the form of educational videos that prompt the sale. They can fill out the purchase form and pay, all without ever talking to a human, making for a fully real-ized marketing pipeline. While these exist for many prod-ucts, they are not easy to create and typically require hiring a funnel marketing expert . . . but when done successfully, they are marketing nirvana.

Another function where marketing and other depart-ments intersect is in establishing a learning management system (LMS). These systems have two functions: external and internal. Starting with internal, the very best companies out there realize the importance of a smooth, integrated onboarding process, because, again, somebody's first day is their most important day.

The best companies schedule LMS time every day during somebody's first week. An automated LMS allows you to set up a computer somewhere in your office for the new hire to watch the many hours of training videos that will educate them on everything they need to get started: company history, product knowledge, technical training, CRM use, filling out contracts, and so forth. It will even provide sales training, teaching them your sales cycle and how to properly sell your products. By delivering all this in an LMS, you can clearly see via the analytics if they watched the training. You can also require tests after each section to evaluate your employees on their knowledge base. Then, at the end, they can get certified, giving them confidence that they know what they need to know. In the executive coaching business I cofounded, I led the team that created over 100 hours of automated onboarding training for new coaches. After completing their LMS training, they knew how to use our CRM, coach to our standards for 26 coaching modules, run workshops, sell to new coaching clients, and more.

Again, the marketing department primarily will be running the development of these learning systems, but we usually bring on consultants to help. We created and staffed a new CRM/LMS unit in IT, featuring people who design LMSs for a living. But your marketing chief typically will be the executive that leads the way when you need a new LMS or a CRM. The marketing team will get quotes from different

CRM providers or consultants, then help decide which is the best fit. The IT side of the house will build exactly the LMS or CRM you request, and marketing should partner with the executive team to create the logic that these systems will perform. That said, as the leader you always need to be aware of all the content, copy, and functions of your CRM or LMS. This is the brain of your business, and nobody will know your business as well as you do. Even if you don't feel like it or you think that it's a waste of time, suck it up and read all the copy on every webpage, click every button in your CRM and LMS, read every automated marketing email, and approve every single marketing blog, podcast, flyer, and sales marketing piece. I promise you will catch things that need to be changed to keep the core messaging of your business heading in the right direction.

The external side of an LMS is client related: It's when you have a product that customers subscribe to that educates them about what you do. We're currently creating one for Totally Mushrooms, where people can pay a monthly fee to receive lessons on how to be a mushroom farmer. The LMS will have different tiers; for instance, automatic access for someone who buys a Totally Mushroom farm, and other access options for nonbuyers who still want superior content on everything to know about growing mushrooms, cooking them, their medicinal benefits, and what the supplements do. We're designing a whole library online and charging money for it because it's valuable. In today's economic climate, you cannot afford to ignore valuable digital marketing and revenue streams.

We also have created an LMS for Tough Stump, our drone

technology and training company for military and first responders. We launched Tough Stump University so they could purchase a certification program called TAK (Team Awareness Kit), where they can plan their missions. This is a training that a large portion of the military and first responders who operate drones and plan missions need to have, and ours is the best. It allowed us to transition from an expensive and not scalable model of in-person training to a very scalable and profitable online automated certification training.

Additionally, we are creating an LMS for SafeSpace Global Corporation (stock ticker SSGC), the global leader in multimodal AI technology that helps save lives. Our chief revenue officer, Theo Davies, is in charge of global expansion, and he is a former Google executive who was their head of sales enablement for all of Asia. He is leading the process for creating a world-class LMS system that will integrate training and certifying our global sales team, and provide training and certification for clients on how to use our AI security systems, for our technicians on how to install our vendors' cameras in which our technology resides, and for our operations team on how to operate all of our technology systems.

Mastering Social Media Marketing

Some executives shy away from social media, probably because they either don't understand it or think it's a waste of time. I once had a consulting client tell me he fired the president of one of his companies because he was using Facebook. How crazy is that?

People are definitely spending time and money on

social media. When properly deployed, a social media strategy is virtually free marketing. If you're not actively engaged in that, then you're missing a huge opportunity. There's a reason that presidents of companies are paying big bucks and blowing up social media. Some of the richest people in the world are the most active on social media. Many well-known billionaires are active on social media. So why would someone running a $1 million company say they don't have time for social media? Elon Musk does, Mark Cuban does, Mark Wahlberg does. Are you busier than Elon Musk? Are you busier than Donald Trump or RFK Jr.? If the most successful leaders in the world are using social media, shouldn't you take time to figure it out?

Leaders find the time for what is important. You therefore need to take some ownership and accept that if you want to get your message out, you must create compelling content and post it. It seems counterintuitive, but who you are personally has a massive impact on your brand, your marketing, and how your audience perceives your company.

Social media marketing is also a very effective recruiting tool, because it can more widely distribute the culture of your company to the world—not only what the company does, but what it's about and why it's important. **People need to see a brand and message over seven times before they remember it.** You want to show people that your company is the best place to work—where the cool people who like to have fun work. Wouldn't you want to work here, too? You don't even have to write copy for the post—a picture or video is worth a thousand words. Whenever you pay for your team to do anything outside of work, even interesting training events, you have a prime opportunity to capture a photo for a post showing why your company is awesome. (Whenever one of the companies I'm leading would go on trips or have events, I became "the photo guy." I am always the one who wants a group photo. I even go as far as bringing my drone everywhere we go and get a very cool-looking aerial shot of the entire team!)

Your social media photos don't have to be as advanced as a drone picture; they can be as simple as a nice smartphone picture. The point is to communicate to the world that your company culture is fun. If I went back and counted how many team members I've recruited from posts like that, it would be dozens. So many of our top people DMed me from a social media post with something like, "This looks like my dream job." Because social media lets the personality of your business come across, it allows people to connect to you in a special way where they feel like they know you.

Another advantage of social media is that it gives you a sampling of what people want. If you post something and no one cares, that's good to know. Instead of spending millions of dollars on some marketing campaign, thinking, "This is the direction we're going to take the company," social media can provide a free test case. Elon Musk does that all the time, and people respond. I'll vote on what SpaceX is going to do next via a Musk post on X.

Similarly, podcasts can do a lot of heavy lifting when it comes to establishing and maintaining an online presence, helping people get to know you, putting your brand out there, establishing and testing messaging, creating community around your brand, and a lot more. My podcast, *All*

Things New Ventures, allows me to build the brand, connect with other business leaders and experts, provide value to my listeners, and cultivate trust and relationships with a broader audience. It takes time and a bit of money to produce, and you have to be consistent in posting frequently, but it's well worth the return we get in interest, engagement, and opportunities that grow from the podcast and our online presence.

It's similar to business development; you've got to stay engaged. You can't have the mindset of "My marketing team does the marketing." The most successful people in the world are very much engaged in their marketing, but they also have teams of people helping them behind the scenes. Someone like President Trump has a whole social media team working on his engagement in the background, but at the end of the day, he's deciding, "I'm gonna post this." It's about a balance between the two. Don't miss out on social media marketing, even if it costs you some time and money. It's all about creating systems that enable you to exploit the most effective means of growth.

Nurturing Customer Relationships Through Marketing

As discussed earlier, most marketing comes down to the funnel—in the CRM, where it all lives. Marketing funnels to sales, to legal, to finance, to service, and then back again to fresh leads. Marketing cannot be a silo, despite its tendency to become one. Even if marketing people are some of the most creative people in your company, marketing needs to be integrated with sales, ops, finance, and every other department. Salesforce or other CRMs can help integrate these things into your LMS, where it serves as the brain of much of the company's sales and marketing. Automate as much as possible—the LMS can help you do this, both externally and internally. Recalling my Tough Stump University example, we have a fully automated sales system where someone can click a website link on social media, watch a sales funnel for TAK-U certification, pay for it online, then receive the LMS content and certification—all automated!

These kinds of strategies apply to all different types of marketing, just as there are strategic principles that apply to all sports. Ultimately, the brand, the team, the message, the media, and the systems are all geared toward the same thing: creating, nurturing, and maintaining a relationship with your audience, and then your customers, that improves their lives and grows your company. That is what Marketing Strategy is designed to do: Begin, maintain, and cultivate valuable relationships with your customers.

The ultimate marketing tool is a customer testimonial. Hopefully if you are doing all the right things outlined so far in this book, your customers will be raving fans. **Getting your raving fans to talk about how great their experience has been working with you, documenting what they say, then packaging the testimonial in ways that compel others to buy from you is pure marketing gold.** Creating a process for getting your customers to give you testimonials, capturing them, and then packaging them should be a core focus of your marketing strategy. Start with simply writing down what customers say when they give you a compliment, then ask, "Do you mind if I publicly share what you just said?" The next level is to hire a videographer or a video marketing company to create three to five customer testimonial videos for your website, social media channels, or automated emails and sales PowerPoint tools.

In summary, your Marketing Strategy needs to encompass the following:

- Creating all your marketing brand identities
- Crafting your marketing and sales materials
- Collaborating on creating your sales and marketing systems and tools
- Capturing your customer testimonials proactively
- Reaching out constantly to your internal and external team members by keeping your brand and marketing active in the world
- Creating leads, which ultimately grow the business

APPLYING MARKETING STRATEGY TO YOUR WORLD

SafeSpace Global, before I initiated a global rebrand, rename, and completely different go-to-market marketing strategy as company president, was called Healthcare Integrated Technologies. Its focus was on selling to senior living facilities and using government grants to pay for installing our amazing multimodal AI technology. The problem was that senior living is one of the most regulated industries in America, right behind nuclear energy, so accessing government grants is a long and drawn-out process. The company was completely out of money to invest in new people, marketing, or updating the products.

The first strategy we deployed was understanding the company's vision, mission, and values, along with how it marketed its offerings. To that end, I drove to a senior living facility in rural Tennessee that had installed our patented multimodal AI software. I was blown away with its effectiveness. It could sign me in, track me in the building, and launch an investigation with the push of a button if something were to happen. The vice president of the facility told me that by using our software, what used to take him eight hours to report for an investigation now took him eight minutes.

I then met my company's CEO and CTO in Knoxville and broke down the custom solutions we created for this client into definable, replicable product offerings. We then reverse-engineered our cost structure and created a sales commission plan and a high-level business plan and vision. Then we mapped out a pricing structure for all the product offerings.

Next, I hired a seasoned sales representative to test our go-to-market strategy. After several months of testing, we discovered that our products were not only appealing to senior living facilities but also to schools, transportation, and commercial buildings as well. We decided to broaden our offerings and expand our vision from just helping save lives in the senior living space to doing so worldwide.

One issue we needed to solve was our company name. "Healthcare Integrated Technologies" presented a disconnect when selling to schools and transportation systems. We decided to hard-pivot and rename, rebrand, and recast the company's entire vision. We changed the company name to SafeSpace Global Corporation and changed the website to www.safespaceglobal.ai. We updated the company vision to "The global leader in multimodal AI technology" and our mission to "We help save lives." We also created our core values:

Have Fun
Integrity
Technology That Matters
Customers First

These strategic marketing changes propelled us to the next level. We went from a team of four people to over 50 in less than nine months. We had more people from different vertices interested in our products than our team had time to meet with. What made all the difference? Gaining clarity on what we do; understanding our market potential; and realigning our marketing strategy with our vision, mission, and values.

Ask yourself these questions:

- On a scale of 1–10, how well does your brand align with your vision, mission, and values?
- If someone interviewed all your team members, how many would be able to state your vision, mission, and values?
- If someone interviewed your customers, how many would be able to state your vision, mission, and values?
- How do you measure the success of your marketing strategy?

- Do you have a lead generation system?
- Do you take ownership of your marketing and brand as a leader and recognize the significance of focusing and investing into it?
- Do you personify your brand and represent it as a leader?

_____

_____

_____

_____

_____

_____

_____

_____

_____

FINANCIAL STRATEGY: ALIGNING YOUR STRENGTHS WITH OPPORTUNITIES

Once you know who you are, strategically build a team that reflects your values, and start scaling your model through tried and tested business development and marketing practices, only a few pieces to the capacity puzzle remain. The last two major pieces, or Pillars, that you need to scale your company, cross the bridge from entrepreneur to true CEO, and, most importantly, increase your capacity, are so intertwined that you can hardly talk about one without the other: Financial Strategy and Legal Strategy.

Financial Strategy is all about using the resources at your disposal. Here are a few examples:

- Forging banking relationships
- Leveraging future cash flow

- Creating financial partners
- Establishing lines of credit
- Creating an equity plan

All these financial tools are designed to grow your business in ways that you couldn't do by simply operating your business on a cash basis. In other words, **you are using your strengths to leverage financial options and take advantage of opportunities that seem out of reach when simply using the cash available day to day.** There are lots of ways to do this, and for many entrepreneurs, Financial Strategy is going to look completely different depending on their stage of growth. This chapter offers some common guidelines and strategies that can help you leverage your strengths and minimize your weaknesses regardless of your company's current size and scale.

FINANCIAL STRATEGY OVERVIEW

Financial strategy is the ability to leverage your natural resources, assets, and brand while reducing your risk, exposure, and liabilities. In essence, you are strategically aligning your strengths with opportunities and minimizing your weaknesses to curtail their development into liabilities.

I was in a meeting recently with a set of potential partners. Everyone was excited about working together, and a range of options were on the table: acquisition, joint venture, cobranding, and others. If I hadn't interrupted this very positive conversation to get us focused on the next steps of looking at the financial dynamics of the potential partnership, that phone call would have gone on for hours, and all we would have done was sing "Kumbaya" to each other. Then the meeting would end, and we would share pleasantries and then set up another meeting to talk more! Maybe, if we were lucky, in the next meeting we'd have one mention of how our partnership might work financially.

I've seen this process go on for months. This is usually the result of a lack of financial knowledge. Neither one of the CEOs on the call knew exactly how to communicate the variety of financial options a partnership can include. **Knowledge breeds confidence, and having the proper possible financial structures in your mind when you're talking to people makes the conversations more tangible and concrete.** Developing your knowledge of financial strategy will save you massive amounts of time. By truly understanding the process and not just doing something out of ignorance (even with positive intent), you'll set yourself up for a successful future partnership.

Most entrepreneurs are ignorant of financial literacy, but not because they're stupid; they just haven't familiarized themselves with a new set of skills. Learning about different financial structures will help grow their business. Plenty of businesses don't have a financial strategy. The executives don't know how to leverage contracts, mergers and acquisitions, or joint ventures (which also involve Legal Strategy), nor how to leverage equity by offering it to people rather than cash compensation.

What does it look like to leverage Financial Strategy to grow your capacity as an entrepreneur?

GETTING IT WRONG: WEBVAN FAILS TO DELIVER

Webvan, a grocery delivery start-up born in the middle of what would become the dot-com bubble, wanted to revolutionize the grocery delivery market with online ordering and doorstep delivery. The company, founded by Louis Borders of Borders Bookstores, had almost $800 million of investment early on. Almost $400 million came from venture capitalists including Sequoia, SoftBank, Goldman Sachs, and Yahoo.[4]

Webvan quickly expanded from its first market in San Francisco to new cities including Sacramento, San Diego, Los Angeles, Chicago, and Seattle. It used $1 billion from its huge cash reserves to build cutting-edge warehouses, costing about $35 million per facility. Webvan spent money much more quickly than they were making it, but its venture capitalists were exerting intense pressure to grow as big as possible, as quickly as possible. With plans to launch in 26 markets within 24 months, building a pricey new warehouse in each market, Webvan bought fleets of vans for grocery deliveries and even started to buy out some of their competitors. All this aggressive expansion came before the model had been fully established in even one market.

Overexpansion driven by intense investor pressure, coupled with an unsustainable business model, led to Webvan's collapse. Unlike today's successful services like Instacart, Webvan built its own expensive infrastructure and failed to get its Financial Strategy right on the front end. Even though Webvan reached the financial goal of many growing companies—an initial public offering that valued the company at several billion dollars—the numbers never made sense.

When Webvan went public in 1999, raising $375 million despite less than $5 million in revenue, the stock doubled in the first day of trading, valuing the company at around $6 billion. Yet 18 months later, you could buy a share of Webvan for $0.06. Webvan spent all its cash, shut down in several markets, and sought millions of dollars more to keep the lights on. In 2001, it failed and shut down completely, but because of its lack of Financial Strategy—including a deal to pay its short-lived CEO hundreds of thousands of dollars annually upon his resignation—Webvan has faded into history.

GETTING IT RIGHT: COSTCO'S FINANCIAL HYPER-GROWTH

Costco operates almost 900 warehouse stores worldwide, employs over 315,000 workers, and exceeds $240 billion in annual revenue, which puts it near the top 10 of all US businesses for total sales. But Costco wouldn't be where it is today without a solid Financial Strategy, which in its early days it executed brilliantly.[5]

In the early 1980s, Costco grew from a concept to a $1 billion company in just three years. Jim Sinegal was a former Price Club executive. Jeffrey Brotman was a lawyer who had a vision of bringing French "hyper-markets" to the United States. In 1983 they opened the first Costco in Seattle. Once they had teamed up, they planned to copy Price Club, Costco's predecessor in many ways, and launched their business in one of the least competitive US markets for grocery retail, the Pacific Northwest.

The first Costco opened as part of a business plan that called for expansion to 12 stores with sales of $80 million per store. By 1985, the company had gone public, and by 1987, Costco hit $1 billion in sales. How did they finance such explosive growth? At first, Sinegal and Brotman bootstrapped with their own funds and credit cards; they were both all-in, risking everything they had for their vision.

Eventually, they raised $7.5 million, enough money to open three warehouses within a year. Most of that money was theirs, or from friends and acquaintances. At the time, $7.5 million seemed like all they would need for their vision. After that, as the company grew, they used investment bankers to help raise money. They kept their salaries low while offering people and businesses what they wanted at prices they needed. It was tough, but they made sacrifices.

As they convinced manufacturers to sell to them, they grew, becoming such a large distribution channel that vendors couldn't ignore them. They achieved their original business plan of a dozen stores with $80 million in sales each, with an overall goal of becoming a billion-dollar company, in three years. When Walmart announced it was getting into the discount warehouse business with Sam's Club, Costco had to grow quickly to compete with such a formidable retailer. After Costco's first three stores succeeded, they were able to get the right products, but funding was key. They were able to leverage their concept, strategy, cash flow, and growth to access venture capital, which they used wisely. As a result, Costco became not just a "hyper-market," but a "hypergrowth" Financial Strategy success story, from bootstrap to NASDAQ.

BREAKDOWN: FINANCIAL STRATEGY

Financial Strategy includes:

- Your financial models
- The investments you make internally and externally
- Your sustainability plan

Your sustainability plan will often require a CFO, a financial review process, and the almighty budget that becomes your roadmap to financial success.

Financial Models: From Bootstrap to NASDAQ

The most basic element of your financial strategy is understanding different frameworks for accessing money. The first framework most entrepreneurs and business owners start with—including success stories like Microsoft—is what we call "bootstrap." The bootstrap financial strategy is when you are putting in your own capital to get an Employer Identification Number or bank account. You're probably in your garage or home office, scrapping it out to start your business.

Under a bootstrap framework, your financial strategy is "sell more, spend less." At this stage, the only way you will have more money is after you sell something. Some businesses can scale through bootstrapping alone. If that works for you, then that's amazing. But beyond that, there might come a point when it makes sense to leverage your financial resources to do more with what you have. At this stage, your financial strategy needs to be more sophisticated.

Often, when I'm hired to help a new business, their entire cash flow goes into paying their bills. They can't make capital investments, because doing so would take all their cash. If they're only making $100,000 in profit, which is a good little business, it's difficult to think about buying a $200,000 software program that could elevate their small business to being a $10 million company. At this level of potential growth, it makes sense to pursue other financial strategies.

The first option typically is debt, which is when you're getting a line of credit from a bank, and more importantly, creating a banking relationship. Most people understand that they will need a bank account when they start a business, but they think of it as just checking a box. A good practice when you set up your bank account is to identify the highest-level person at the bank, get to know them, and share your business plan with them. Your banker, whether you like it or not, is part of your financial team, and can become an important partner.

When you start using debt instruments as part of your financial strategy, the relationship with your bank is paramount. If the economy is doing well, banks will be freely lending money and you can even get preapproved online; when it isn't doing as well, businesses have more trouble getting credit. This is when the relationship you'd built would ease things, and you could still get a loan to buy a piece of property, make a capital investment, or have a line of credit for increased operating expenses.

A good rule of thumb for a credit line is to have at least six months' worth, if not a full year, of credit for operating

your business. If shit hits the fan, you will be able to keep your business open by using the credit as a debt facility. Companies that do not have a financial strategy will go out of business. Your competitors will close because they don't have dry powder—neither the cash reserves nor the line of credit—to weather the storm. Even if you are cash-flow positive, it's worth having the maximum amount of credit available, even if you don't need to use it; it can serve as a base layer for your Financial Strategy moving forward.

After you're shifting out of bootstrapping and have cash flow, a banking relationship and debt facility, and a line of credit of some sort, the next step to consider is buying property. I believe it's always better to own your business's real estate. You might have to

> A good rule of thumb for a credit line is to have at least six months' worth, if not a full year, of credit for operating your business.

start with leasing an office, but as soon as you can afford it, consider owning the building your business is in. Don't rent when you can own. Unless you're massively in debt, as soon as you have cash flowing and you have some resources, finding a way to own your building is usually a great move. Sometimes it's not feasible, like trying to buy a commercial building in downtown Manhattan. But if you're in, say, Ashland City, Tennessee, you can probably figure out how to buy something to house your business.

Kyah, my wife, did a great job with this for her jewelry business, Sleeveless. She started with the product, literally in our basement. We had a shop set up there where people would come to our house and make jewelry downstairs. Then she bought a Snap-On Tools truck, painted it, retrofitted it, installed a chandelier and glass cases, and began going to events and driving this mobile fashion boutique around. She had a business partner, so half of it was men's clothing and accessories, and the other half was my wife's women's accessories. She also used that truck to sell to other businesses. She ended up getting her stock in 80 different stores across the South.

Then they got to the point where it made sense for them to be retail, so she opened up a shop. She didn't have to start by spending a lot of money to rent 10 different storefronts; instead she bought a truck and sold to other people's storefronts to get the money going, then eventually had her own store. She did that for several years until we had our daughter, then sold her half to her business partner. She was able to build all this value by making sound, strategic financial decisions.

The next level of financial strategy is taking on investors. There are different levels of investors. Angel investors invest in an idea, typically on aggressive terms. These are the investors you pursue if you don't have anything proven and you're pre-revenue; they're going to look at a few different things when you ask them for money: not just you as the entrepreneur, but also your track record as their main metric. Do you have a history of doing the thing that you're asking them for money to do, for which you're going to be able to provide an ROI?

When you approach angel investors, you're communicating, "I have a business plan, and if you give me $300,000, that gives me a year of being able to build this product." Be aware that getting angel investors is hard, especially if you're trying to avoid giving away the whole company before you even start. If you're trying to get an investor to give you a million dollars for 20% of your company, that means you think your company is worth $5 million.

Often in the angel round, you'll ask for $50,000 or $100,000 to just get a proof of concept off the ground. I personally think friends and family are a better option than angel investors because usually they'll do it without asking for half of the company or some other large percent of equity. Most financial advisors will tell you not to take on too many equity investors early.

By contrast, a venture capitalist is an investor who is looking for a business that already has some form of revenue. When you hear people on *Shark Tank* say, "This isn't ready for venture capital yet," they usually mean that the product doesn't have a full year of audited financials. Your business needs enough of a track record to have a true valuation, which a venture capitalist can take to their team and determine what kind of ROI they will get. Venture capital will usually want a controlling interest, so they will buy 51% of your company. They usually will try to negotiate what your multiple is by looking at your EBITDA, which is earnings before interest, taxes, depreciation, and amortization.

If you did $100,000 in EBITDA, they might offer you a 5× multiple for $500,000, but they may want to own 51% of your company. That might be a "no" if you're not ready for that yet and need to get a few things figured out first. It's your clue that you're not ready for venture capital; your EBITDA profit

margins are not high enough to take the multiple they're going to offer.

A third investment option is private equity, which will
sometimes come in for a smaller share (5%–20%) of the
company. You'll see this on things like *Shark Tank* as well.
The difference between venture capital and private equity
is where the money comes from; private equity typically is
somebody's own money, whereas venture capital is using a
pool of other people's money. Say 10 people have given a venture capitalist a million dollars, so they have $10 million to
deploy, and then they've promised those people, "I'm going
to beat the market, and I'm going to give you a 15%–20%
ROI." Venture capitalists have a fiduciary responsibility to
those people to make them as much money as they can while
minimizing risk, and typically they are operating under a
model with an aggressive time horizon to see an ROI on the
capital they deploy. Private equity investors have more flexibility because they're using their own money.

Another important consideration is how much involve-
ment you want from your investors. If you go with venture
capital, they will often just say, "Hit the number and pay us."
This is different from a strategic partner, an investor who
also will come onboard to help you grow your company.

After learning about all the different forms of financial
vehicles, it's time to sit down and put together your Financial Strategy, determining how this could work when you
start your business. For example, you might decide that you
are going to bootstrap it. Determine how much money you
and your business partners have, and how much you think
your family and friends are willing to give. Plan for when the

company's revenue gets to a million, and how you will build a relationship with your bank and establish a line of credit. Then, every year, you can meet with your bank and see if you can get them to increase your credit line. If there is no Financial Strategy and you're just shooting the next target that's right in front of you, then you won't be looking for the opportunity to partner or leverage.

Another area of Financial Strategy is acquiring other businesses. At this stage, your company has enough cash flow to start eyeing your competitors and considering acquisitions and mergers. Instead of simply taking $5 million in profit and spending it on yourself, now you can put that back into the company's growth. If you're aiming to go from $15 million to $100 million in revenue, why not take that $5 million, acquire those smaller competitors, and roll them up into your business?

You know what people do when they don't have a strategy? They pay themselves. They take all $5 million, they sweep it, and then they go buy a $5 million swimming pool, a yacht, or blow the money on something else, and then, a lot of times, they get complacent, because now they're living the lifestyle of the rich and famous. And guess what happens to the business? Either it plateaus or declines and that's what you have for the rest of your life. **The best investment you can make as a business owner is to keep investing into growing your business.** Do not pull the lifeblood "dry powder" out of your business and blow it ... keep doubling down and see how big you can grow what you started!

At this level, the financial and the legal aspects become increasingly intertwined because you're making large deals,

You know what people do when they don't have a strategy? They pay themselves.

negotiating compli-cated contracts, or establishing joint ventures. The more you scale, the more important legal be-comes in financial decisions.

For many business owners, the final stage of Financial Strategy is your exit strategy. Many entrepreneurs build businesses without an exit strategy, but others have an eye from the very beginning on selling at some point. **One important factor in selling your business, being acquired, or merging with another company is maximizing the multiples of your valuation.** Few people think in terms of the multiples of their business. Basing decisions on what's going to increase your multiples is a whole other way of thinking from a Financial Strategy standpoint and a legal standpoint, because there are certain things that investors, banks, and others like that look for. A lot of entrepreneurs have no idea how these supercharge the value of your business. So, what are these aspects?

- Residual revenue models with multiple streams of revenues
- Recurring contracts that go into perpetuity; for example, when dealing with the government, getting programs of record in the military where they buy your products forever
- SAS technology that runs the backbone of a business forever

- IP contracts, patents, trademarks, and copyrights that protect the value of what you've created
- Future growth of the market your business is in
- Measurable and predictable pipeline
- The monthly, quarterly, and annual revenue growth trajectory
- Growing EBITDA and margin
- Strength of the executive team's experience

Certain sectors have higher multiples than others. When you negotiate the Financial Strategy and put that into the legal documents, the multiple from that can be significant. If you're looking to sell your business in the next few years, you must integrate that into your Financial Strategy.

Investing in Your People

When thinking about how you will invest back into your company, one of the largest areas for this is staffing and compensation. You need to map out a strategic staffing growth plan as part of your financial strategy. As the company grows, you'll want your team's incomes to grow, too, so the question of "How are we going to pay people?" should be part of the discussion from the beginning. Part of this is planning out the company's compensation tiers, from entry level to executive. What is the market rate for this type of work in your specific city or state? What phase is your business in and what can you afford? You must consider all of those when putting your Financial Strategy together for your compensation plans.

Then, you can put bonus structures together, and establish pay-increase systems to set proper expectations with top talent (who may accept a haircut financially if they know the upside is potentially there for a big future payoff). Mapping that out as part of your Financial Strategy is important. Additionally, paying yourself as the owner will necessitate a compensation plan as the CEO. I often find this is the area that gets the least attention, and I have to create a compensation plan for the CEO when companies bring me on.

Sustaining Financial Strategy: Teams, Reviews, and the Almighty Budget

We have explored the major components of Financial Strategy that you should be considering. To circle back to the fundamentals of having a great team, having a badass CFO is one of the best investments you can make. Most entrepreneurs who get in the game are primarily focused on engineering, product, IT, or sales. Maybe they're really good at selling and have a passionate, solid vision. They have an Integrator who's good at creating a product or an IT system. But they don't have a CFO to manage cash flow or create and update a P&L and balance sheet. Many times, they're just trying to do the books on their own, or they ask their sister, who knows how to use Excel, to be their financial person and pay the bills and do payroll. They do not have a proper CPA or a CFO involved. Often the excuse is "We cannot afford a CFO." If you can't afford a CFO, get a part-time fractional CFO. Without a monthly financial review where you are looking at your P&L, balance sheet, and cash summary—and comparing the actuals to your budget and prior year—you are flying blind as a business leader.

A major part of your Financial Strategy that will involve your CFO is ensuring that financial reviews are taking place. What you need as a business leader, strategically, is the tool that encompasses all of your Financial Strategy: the financial review. This review should happen every single month,

Having a badass CFO is one of the best investments you can make.

no matter what. You also want to have a financial team, typically composed of the CEO and the CFO or another head of money, treasurer, controller, or the like. The COO is often involved, maybe the head of sales, and any other key executives driving the business decisions—typically a small group of your key decision makers. These stakeholders meet once a month to review a financial package.

A financial package typically contains a monthly P&L statement listing what you did that month compared to what your budget was and to your performance that month the year prior. How much revenue did you do in each product line item? How much money did you spend on each product line item, and what does it total? These are the questions you review. You look at it month by month, and then you look at it year to date, compared to both the budget and the prior year. That's the high-level view of what a P&L should look like.

In addition, your financial package includes your balance sheet, which is different from the P&L and helps you manage your cash. What are your accounts receivable and accounts payable, and how much cash is literally in the bank that you can make payroll with? A lot of times, owners and CEOs are so transfixed by just paying their bills that they're not getting outside of that box and seeing the larger strategic landscape. Their biggest point of stress is managing the cash of the business. Offloading that task to a true CFO, though, and deploying some of the strategies I've discussed, like getting a line of credit and working capital, can be a CEO's biggest stress reliever while increasing their capacity.

Establishing the budget—and holding to it—is also part of the Financial Strategy. A great way to manage your business is just to say, **when someone asks you if they can spend money, "Well, is it in the budget?" And if it is, then great; it's not an emotional decision. "Yeah, let's do it." If it's not, you can answer, "Yeah, you know, we can't right now." Otherwise you have to "steal from Peter to pay Paul."** If you can't work within the lines of your budget, eventually you'll run out of money. At the end of the day, your financial team, instruments, and strategy have to be implemented, and holding to your budget is the primary way to make that happen.

APPLYING FINANCIAL STRATEGY TO YOUR WORLD

When I started at Healthcare Integrated Technologies (which, as mentioned, we renamed SafeSpace Global Corporation), we were completely out of money. Our CEO and founder, Scott Boruff, personally paid my first paycheck to bring me on. The first objective Scott tasked me with was to create a marketing plan to raise capital and provide the resources needed to grow and scale. I created my first ever investor pitch deck and started making calls. When we first started raising capital, the share value of the company's stock—trading over the counter at the time—was $0.06, and the market cap of the company was $7 million. After several failed attempts, we finally got our first investor for $200,000! We successfully raised our first million dollars through one-on-one presentations, but it was a grind. We then created an investor presentation called "Bootstrap to New York Stock Exchange" and delivered it to a group of around a dozen people. From that meeting we raised another several hundred thousand dollars and developed our marketing scripts to inform investors how they can get involved in SafeSpace Global without having to travel to meet them one-on-one. We now had a scalable financial fundraising strategy.

Using the Bootstrap to New York Stock Exchange presentation, we started hosting both in-person events and webinars and successfully raised another $2 million, for a total of $3 million raised in three months! Not bad for my first time raising capital.

As our business plan evolved, we created a compensation and installation model to help speed our business development and marketing strategy. We realized we'd need to raise an additional $2 million to ensure the run-rate needed to execute our aggressive business plan of reaching a $1 billion valuation in five years. I recommended we create a fundraising strategy that would leverage our existing investor base, who had already invested $3 million into the company, by activating them to invest more and/or attract other investors with the goal of raising a total of $5 million invested. We created a SafeSpace Global Summit event where all 20 or so team members from across the world flew into Nashville for a world-class three-day training event. The highlight was a "meet the team" VIP event, where we invited all of our current and potential investors to a catered experience where they were able to meet one another as well as our entire newly recruited, first-class sales and operations team. We then cohosted a VIP dinner of more than 30 people in a private dining room. I asked every investor to stand up with a microphone and share with the group "why I am excited to be an investor in SafeSpace." Despite being optional, 29 out of 30-plus investors stood up and shared their testimonials. It was amazing! Several people got emotional when talking about being aligned with our mission to help save lives. Many people passionately affirmed how much they believe in our world-class team. It was an awesome event.

The result was unbelievable. The day after the event, both Scott and I were overwhelmed with inbound requests to invest more money in our Friends & Family round. There was no way possible to schedule everyone who was interested, so at 10:30 PM we decided to host a webinar for the next day. We had approximately 30 people show up for the webinar midday on a Friday. There were so many people who invested from that call and told their friends, we had to host *another* webinar on Saturday for around the same number of attendees.

At this point neither Scott nor I knew most of the people on the call who wanted to invest. We had successfully expanded our financial strategy beyond our friends and family and it was organically taking off. Another amazing by-product started happening as a result of these financial strategy maneuvers: friends of friends of friends started talking about this amazing new AI tech company focused on saving lives, and the publicly traded stock started taking off! Again, when I had started with the company six months prior the stock was trading at six cents per share; it ended up going to $0.47 per share with a market cap value of over $40 million! After the smoke settled from this mind-blowing financial strategy to raise $5 million, we ended up successfully raising $10 million! We now had more than enough capital to deploy our $1 billion business plan, but we could also skip into investing in more advanced AI and looking into M&A expansion opportunities to grow our product offerings. (For more information about SafeSpace Global Corporation, go to our website at www.SafeSpaceGlobal.AI, call your stockbroker, or go to your E*TRADE app and search for our OTC stock ticker at "SSGC.")

What is your financial strategy? Do you have a scheduled monthly financial review? If so, are you reviewing an updated P&L and balance sheet using generally accepted accounting principles (GAAP)? When reviewing your financial deck, do you have it organized by actuals for the current month, prior month, and year to date, then compare it to current-month and year-to-date budgets? Also, are you hosting a weekly cash management meeting and reviewing your balance sheet, and do you have a 13-week rolling cash forecasting tool to manage the financial strategy of your business?

If you answered "No, I wish!" to these questions, ask

yourself if your current financial team is able to build the preceding tools and present them to you in a professional way, to help you make data-based decisions in your monthly financial reviews. If not, what do you need to do to recruit the right team to make all the above a reality?

Don't let fear stop you from doing any of this. There is no other position in your company more important than a competent, reliable, game-changing CFO. If you cannot afford such a CFO, my challenge to you is that you cannot afford *not* to have a CFO help you find the money to pay for themselves. You might need to replace your current financial chief with just such a pro. Replacing team members is difficult, but no one ever said being a leader is easy.

LEGAL STRATEGY: NAVIGATING THE LAWS OF BUSINESS

The fifth and last Strategic Pillar is Legal Strategy. No matter how great your Executive, Business Development, Marketing, and Financial Strategies are, they will need legal protections and structures to sustain your long-term growth. The larger and more productive a business becomes, the more it bumps into the laws of the land, whether those are regulations, contracts, or necessary relationships with governing authorities. Local, state, national, and even international law become an ever greater concern as you grow. For all these reasons, you need to develop your Legal Strategy as soon as possible.

Although they are separate functions, Financial Strategy and Legal Strategy are difficult to discuss independently. When making certain important decisions or transactions, you must consider both the legal and financial sides of the situation, often simultaneously. Typically, these two pillars come together most clearly in contracts. Contracts usually will be crafted by a lawyer, but the details within the contract are usually coming from the financial strategist or the executive team, who are enacting the financial strategy. It is rare to find a lawyer that has given me any good ideas about financial strategy whatsoever. People commonly make the mistake, when they don't know what to do, of thinking, "My lawyer is a smart guy." So then they ask their lawyer for Financial Strategy advice, which most of the time is like asking a CPA for legal advice. Nevertheless, you do need to consider these strategies in concert, with the right team in place, as you continue to scale and grow your capacity.

LEGAL STRATEGY OVERVIEW

At most levels of business, lawyers are a necessity. Part of your Legal Strategy, though, is to know what tasks or roles lawyers tend to excel in, and what tasks are better left to the financial team or other members of your executive team. **When lawyers draft a contract, they are setting and enforcing the rules for the race. They are making sure everything follows legal procedure. But you, the leader, are the one driving. It's your words and your strategy; you are not asking the lawyer to map out the strategy for you.** Remember my point about assuming your lawyer is smart. They are, but don't assume this expertise applies to everything. The reason they're lawyers is likely because they enjoy law and process, which is different from the high-risk world of entrepreneurs. Many lawyers (not all) are probably intimidated by the prospect of being entrepreneurs and doing risky things like mergers and acquisitions.

GETTING IT WRONG: NO CONTRACT, NO LEVERAGE

One company I work with had a significant liability with one of our manufacturing partners. Our CEO had a brilliant idea to call this manufacturer, which manufactured 90% of a certain kind of technology worldwide. He saw people using it to track

> It's your words and your strategy; you are not asking the lawyer to map out the strategy for you.

things, and had the idea to retrofit it, allowing their technology to track everything from drones to dogs to people. Even better, it provides tracking for many things on one screen in all weather and conditions. The CEO approached the executives at the manufacturer and said, "If you'll create this retrofitted product for me, I'll sell the socks off of it." And he did.

They shook hands, created a pricing sheet, and that was the only document. The only thing we had in writing for this valuable product-creation and manufacturing relationship was that pricing sheet they emailed us. Eventually, this product became the number one revenue generator for the whole company, and that's when I found out about the total lack of long-term legal strategy. There were no contracts, yet the manufacturer was missing its deadlines. The missed deadlines became a problem, then a liability; it was reflecting on our business, even if the root problem wasn't our fault. Not only that—we decided to increase our prices, as we were not making the margin needed to successfully keep selling this amazing tracker. Once the manufacturer found out we were increasing our prices, they increased *their* pricing to eat up all the margin gain we were hoping to use to grow our business.

The reality was that without a contract, we had no leverage with the manufacturer for anything. They almost had more leverage on *us* because they just needed a seller; they were creating the product, so they could have massively screwed us over by finding someone else to sell it to the military. As soon as I got wind of this, we booked a meeting with all the stakeholders of the manufacturer. We flew out west for almost two days of meetings and tours. Over one four-hour strategic session, we hammered out the current relationship, how we understand it, and what the future possibilities could be. We concluded that we were entertaining two options: a joint venture or a master operations agreement. After constructive conversations over the next several months, and explaining practically what a joint venture does, they agreed that they wanted a contract just as much as we did. Several follow-up phone calls later, we had lawyers map out how a joint venture could work. We also reviewed what a master manufacturing agreement could look like. We ended up creating a win-win manufacturing agreement that protects both companies and secures the value we are building together.

The moral of the story: You need contracts to ensure a fair relationship and outcomes for the long-term sustainability and growth of your business.

GETTING IT RIGHT: BECOMING INTEGRATED

As mentioned, I recently became president and CSO for SafeSpace Global Corporation, the global leader in helping save lives with patented AI technology. Our product monitors at-risk elderly people using facial recognition software and alerts caretakers and family members if they leave the senior living facility or some other event occurs to put them at risk. Scott Boruff, our CEO, has raised over $1 billion on Wall Street and is an expert at taking companies public on the over-the-counter (OTC) market. An OTC company is publicly traded, and anyone can buy stocks in it; these trades are less centralized than those on NASDAQ or the New York Stock Exchange. Scott uses a strategy called a "reverse triangle merger" to acquire a publicly traded OTC company, modify and grow it, up-list them to NASDAQ, and then to the NYSE. Acquisitions are a common strategy he uses; for example, he took the last oil and gas company he acquired and ran from around $0.10 to $9.00 a share.

Intertwined financial and legal dynamics work together in these deals to achieve a higher goal. Scott sends a letter of intent to a company he wants to acquire, then he raises money by calling investors and having them buy stock through a subscription agreement, in which someone sells stock at a set price that requires the buyer to hold it for a set period before selling. He then uses the cash from these investments to acquire the company, which becomes part of his conglomerate; this accretive purchase causes the stock price to rise. For this reason, Scott often acquires using stock rather than cash, which will multiply return for those business owners as the stock values rise, once the deal goes through. This is a kind of mini–Berkshire Hathaway model.

You have to implement your legal and financial strategies intentionally, in tandem, to accomplish this kind of growth. Your subscription agreement needs to be dialed in; the structure of the company needs to be carefully maintained by a team of lawyers and accountants; and you need audited financials (GAAP accounting), a clean P&L, and a growing balance sheet to be acquired. Everything needs to be integrated for these kinds of strategies to work. Overall, investing with a publicly traded company has some advantages, one being that they've already been audited. This can make these investments more secure than private ventures; the financial due diligence helps the effectiveness of your Legal Strategy.

BREAKDOWN: LEGAL STRATEGY

Legal Strategy applies to several different areas of your business, including:

- Mergers and acquisitions
- Contracts

Remember, the more growth you experience, the more areas of your business will be significantly affected by your Legal Strategy, or lack of it.

Mergers and Acquisitions

Like most entrepreneurs, when you start considering mergers, acquisitions, or strategic partnerships, you may be a fish out of water. You start getting into something that's very industry or business specific, or very financially complex, or a transaction that requires a strategic plan. This is when you get the lawyers involved. I repeat: You must have a lawyer for M&A, unless you have a legal degree . . . and you probably still want to hire a lawyer for selling or acquiring a business. You also have to be really careful about reading contracts, as they can be difficult to parse without the help of a legal professional. In any case, when it comes to mergers and acquisitions, you need experienced, skilled lawyers on your team to make sure that everything is buttoned up.

For instance, at the end of one successful meeting, where we were considering a whole range of options including acquisition, we agreed that we were not going to hold the intellectual property (IP) jointly. We'd already discussed having the other company own it.

However, consider what might happen, as the deal was being agreed to, if the CEO had forgotten to say that. Sometimes no one even thinks to bring such a detail up, because it's "obvious" to both sides. That's why you need a lawyer to be part of that discussion.

Such an omission can end up being one of those things,

way down the road, that blows everything up. In our case, had a lawyer not been part of the discussion, the CEO would have decided that we, solely, were going to own this IP. And then this would have gone in the contract. Then our CEO would have trusted the lawyer and failed to read the contract carefully, and when it went to the other company, they'd see it and it would be a total trustbuster. Momentum stops. The reality is, by letting our lawyer make the decisions, our CEO wouldn't have had a Legal Strategy going into the negotiation. To craft such a strategy, he would need to think through all the pieces and parts of the deal, the things someone would want to have as part of the legal negotiation. I've seen this happen more than once. A proposal with perceived egregious terms, conditions, or language can blow up a deal.

So besides having your lawyer in the room, how should you approach your Legal Strategy? As mentioned, the number one rule of your Legal Strategy is to integrate it with your Financial Strategy. Although they are separate, you have to keep your financial considerations in mind. What are your objectives? What are your possibilities for how a business structure could work, whether it's designed to increase revenue or branch out strategically? **Whether you're buying new assets, developing a new business, reducing liabilities, paying down debt, consolidating credit, or selling off unprofitable segments of the business to help your multiple for your valuation, Legal and Financial Strategy have to work together—and much of the time, that Financial Strategy will drive the Legal Strategy.** This is especially true of mergers and acquisitions.

Contracts

In general, a lawyer will attempt to translate your needs accurately when drafting a contract. Most of the lawyers I know are nice, kind, and considerate, but they are not always big-picture, strategic people. So when they're trying to translate something complex that you've said to them into language that makes sense in a contract, even a lawyer with the best of intentions can totally lose its context and quash the spirit and intent of the negotiation. I've encountered this, and I know dozens of entrepreneurs who have too. Lawyers are thinking about legal requirements, which can often misconstrue the "spirit" of the agreement. Many successful CEOs have fallen into this ditch.

As noted earlier, the one rule you should abide by in all your legal decisions is simple: Sit down and read the contract. Actually spend the time, without distractions, to go over what you're signing. It's crucial if you're early on as an entrepreneur, and you are making your way to becoming a CEO, that you as the leader read every contract you sign. And don't just read it—sit down with a big glass of water and focus. Every beginning entrepreneur needs to understand this. You cannot be distracted, and you need to be thinking actively. I used to be that charismatic CEO visionary who just trusted my lawyers and my CFOs, and I knew all the people around me were smart enough to take what I said and put it into a contract accurately, and get it right. Sometimes I was wrong.

After the tenth time this kind of thing went poorly, from losing acquisitions to having people quit, I discovered that many of the contracts I'd received were wildly different from what I had communicated to Legal. Whether you wrote it or not, a contract will reflect on your intentions as a leader.

> The one rule you should abide by in all your legal decisions is simple: Sit down and read the contract. Actually spend the time, without distractions, to go over what you're signing.

After literally losing acquisitions and partnerships and almost having people quit because they read what was in the contract and it was way different from what we had discussed, I knew it reflected on me as a leader, and I knew it had to change.

If your contract doesn't reproduce what you discussed with people, they will think you're trying to screw them. They will assume that you, as the CEO or other leader, told a lawyer to put this weird wording over here, and you made something seem arbitrary over there. You're the one who made it vague or one sided, and now the relationship is in danger. Contracts can often come off as one sided because your lawyer, while not trying to screw over the other party, will work to have your back and line things up to be in favor of their client. They're just thinking, "Well, I'm just going to make this favor my client's interest."

These types of errors can occur because of simple miscommunication. When you meet with the other party and review all the details of the agreement, the lawyer might not be present. Lawyers work from what you communicate and might not understand that you agreed with the other party to certain conditions. If you forget to fully explain the agreement to your lawyer, and then don't carefully review the contract, it might not accurately reflect your goals—even if it was a really big deal. Just as with mergers and acquisitions, any kind of contract can be sabotaged when Legal Strategy (and the actual lawyer) isn't integrated into everything else.

Strategic Contract Negotiations

This might seem like I'm repeating myself, but it's extremely important to have your team aligned when you enter any kind of strategic negotiation. Otherwise, it's easy for the entire process to become siloed. You might be blazing ahead, meeting with owners and CEOs, making progress on the perfect deal, but you also might be agreeing to commitments you're unable to fulfill—and unknowingly disadvantaging yourself. Always have your lawyer or legal team present from the onset of negotiations. Even if an agreement makes sense in terms of your financial goals, you may be committing to something different from what you initially envisioned—or even something illegal. Lawyers can usually nip these issues in the bud before they become larger problems. It's better to have Legal in on the negotiation from the start than to try to incorporate them afterward.

You can be the greatest negotiator in the world, you can take all the seminars and read all the books you want, and you can have an advanced knowledge of game theory, and any negotiation can still go sideways or blow up if you don't know the law. Have an expert on your team who really understands the rules, and why they are there in the first place.

APPLYING LEGAL STRATEGY TO YOUR WORLD

As CSO of Tough Stump Technologies, I identified Legal Strategy as a huge opportunity to increase the value of the company, specifically its contracts and agreements with internal team members as well as outside manufacturers, vendors, and strategic partners. None of the executive team at Tough Stump were lawyers; they had spent 25-plus years in Special Operations providing Tier 1 service to our country, then another 8 years building Tough Stump. As a result, the agreements that were in place were built on trust, but not binding or legally protected from unfortunate events.

We engaged an amazing legal professional to help guide us and went to work on our Legal Strategy. Internally, we started looking at everyone's contracts, positions, compensation plans, and equity structure. Starting at the top, the first recommendation I made was for the cofounder, who had become CFO out of necessity, to replace himself as CFO and become COO. At first he was not happy to hear this recommendation, but he eventually agreed it was the right call. I personally recruited the new CFO and helped negotiate her contract and agreement.

Next, we looked at some of the company's retention issues. Its lack of an internal equity opportunity had given the competition the opportunity to poach key people. I brought in a world-class legal team to help create a new equity structure to realize the vision the CEO, Jarrett "Fish" Heavenston, had for his team to own a piece of the business and be rewarded for their dedication to building the business. Additionally, we reworked the entire company compensation and bonus structure to help motivate people to be Tough Stumpers for life.

Then we looked at our vendor and manufacturing agreements. We needed to add residual contracts and IP protection rights to the amazing technology, services, training, and tracking products the company had created. Our legal counsel helped us navigate putting together a win-win agreement that protects the IP for both companies and adds value to both businesses.

Does your general counsel or legal team give you strategic advice to help grow the value of the company, or do they focus only on defensive measures? Do you personally know what the terms and conditions are for your employees' contracts? For your clients' contracts? For your vendors'? Have you built protections into your contracts that protect your workforce from getting raided if a disgruntled team member leaves and tries to take people with them? Do you have protections for your IP if a vendor decides to go into the same business as you? Do your contracts have clauses to protect the company from clients stealing your team away?

How often are you engaging your legal team? Do you run ideas by them to preempt legal snares? When opening a new market or product line, do you include your legal team in the conversation to help guide the development of the new idea so it conforms to the legal parameters needed to be successful?

If you answered, "I wish I had someone to help me with all of these things," it's time to put a search together and go find yourself an amazing legal partner to help increase your capacity and help grow your business bigger than you.

OPTIMAL CAPACITY: STRATEGIC WISDOM FOR YOUR WHOLE LIFE

The Five Pillars will give you the strategic tools and capacity you need to build the bridge from being an entrepreneur to becoming a true, optimized CEO. Once you have Executive, Business Development, Marketing, Financial, and Legal strategies in place, you will eliminate most of the causes of business failure; the natural result of this advanced level of strategic alignment is growth. Your capacity will continue to grow with each step you take along this path, and I am confident that your business endeavors will succeed.

The problem is that success in business is never enough. There are a lot of successful leaders, founders, owners, and CEOs out there who, despite all their success, are still miserable. While this book is about capacity as an entrepreneur, to reach the highest possible level of your life—your Optimal

Capacity—you need a whole-life strategy with lessons and wisdom that apply to your life inside and outside of your business. Innovation in your work life, clarity in how you analyze macroeconomic and political events, professional sustainability, personal growth, family life, balance, ability to overcome challenges, learning and flexibility, mindfulness, and core leadership principles—all of these contribute to who you are, how you live and work, and the kind of person you are becoming.

Here, we harness the strategic power of the Pillars for every area of life, to help you, as a whole person, reach your Optimal Capacity.

INNOVATIVE STRATEGIES FOR OPTIMAL CAPACITY

This is not a book for everyone, so I don't want to lose focus here toward the end by portraying it as a general self-help book. Rather, this is a book for entrepreneurs and leaders who are serious about building things that will last: companies and brands that employ people, make life better, and contribute to the world at scale. To do this, obviously you will need the strategic Pillars, but those Pillars naturally lead to some more specific ideas that will supercharge your capacity and growth, including leveraging cutting-edge technology, continually innovating the sustainability of your business model, and navigating the latest cultural trends and issues that will, like it or not, improve your business moving forward.

Learn Artificial Intelligence Tools

Artificial intelligence has already changed the world. There's no going back to a time before AI; the genie is out of the bottle. If you're not learning how to be a professional prompter who can skillfully harness AI in your everyday workflows, other people in your field will, and they're going to be the ones with jobs in the future. The people who fear AI, the ones who are not learning how to use it, are going to get left in the dust.

Now **I don't think that AI is going to rule the world. It's going to be humans who know how to leverage AI who, in the very near future, will rule the world.** Harness it today. It will save you time, effort, energy, frustration, and money. Most of what people have been doing from the 1950s until very recently, AI can do for you at a fraction of the time and cost. I can't count the number of times a week I'm pulling up ChatGPT and having it create something for me that I normally would have had to pay another human to create: financial forecasts, PowerPoints, job descriptions, business plans, compensation packages, blogs, prospecting lists . . . and much, much more. All you need to do is speak, and it does all the work. Even dictation, taking handwritten notes and typing them for you; the things ChatGPT, Grok, Gemini, and other popular large language model (LLM) AI programs are doing is amazing!

Last, because most industries at some point involve reading and writing, even the most traditional industries (like farming, manufacturing, taxi driving, restaurant service, bartending . . . and more!) can be transformed by using these kinds of cutting-edge tools. Think about how you can increase your capacity by harnessing AI and do it today. Buy in fully, and don't let fear keep you from growing. Make yourself an expert in AI, for your industry, and your value will skyrocket.

Ensure Your Business Models Are Sustainable

Innovation is great, but as we've covered throughout this book, to build something that lasts, you need to build on a solid foundation. Think of this as a microcosm of some of the most important fundamental ideas we've covered. Remember these core questions:

- Does the product matter?
- Are there macroeconomic tailwinds for the industry and product you're selling?
- Are you on the front of the macroeconomic wave and adapting to innovations such as AI?
- Look at top people in the industry; are you a student of the game?
- Reverse-engineer what the best companies do; are you taking the best and leaving the rest (without stealing)?
- Are you collecting best practices?
- Have you created your business model on paper, including pricing and go-to-market strategy (sales)?
- Have you thought about the team you need, engaged a financial person and an Integrator (for operations), and filled out the rest of your team structure?

- Are you using equity if you don't have money, or borrowing money, to execute a business plan and attract talented people?

To put more meat on these questions: Back in 2007, when I was starting the coaching business as the industry was just coming together, I would ask people, "Do you have a business coach?" And they would say, "What's a business coach?" Well, fast-forward ten years. By 2017, I was asking, "Do you have a business coach?" And they would say either, "I've had one or my best friend has one" or "I've been thinking about getting one." So, the market became educated about what business coaching was. We were at the front end of that wave and had a successful ride.

The beginning wave of a new economic development and macro trend is the ideal time to start your business. Once you know you're in the right pond to fish in, you need to put a plan together. After you identify what you want to do, start looking at the top people in the industry to figure out how they are doing it. How are they going to market? What's their price point? How are they selling it? Become a student of the game and try to reverse-engineer their processes. You don't have to reinvent the wheel each time, but this does not mean you can steal people's intellectual property. If there's a best practice that's commonly used and accepted, learn from it and then start creating your business model from there. Actually put it on paper and consider what the product is going to be. How much are you going to charge? What's going to be included? How are you going to sell it? What's your go-to market strategy? How are you going to prospect? How are you going to present it? How are you going to charge for it?

Next, think of your team. Who do I need to have in each position in the company? You need the sales, vision, passion, go-getter, business development person, the financial person, an operations person, and then you can start filling out your company organizational chart and staffing further based on the needs of your company. If it's a tech company, you need to bring on a key person around tech who does programming, knows how to build a tech team, build a tech stack, and so forth. When you're starting and you have no money, all you have is equity. So out of the gates, you just say, "Hey, we're going to build this thing. It's going to be huge. We're going to do 10 million, 100 million, a billion dollars. And if you help me take this idea into reality, I'd like to make you an X percent partner." So you can give out equity in the early days if you don't have money, or you can go get money by finding a really rich person and presenting the idea to them—"Hey, would you mind funding this idea?"—instead of bootstrapping the idea. Once you have that seed money, you can execute your business plan.

So, once you have your basic strategies figured out, what makes it sustainable? If you are on your way to answering my questions about starting your business, then you have a foundation. But to make it sustainable, remember that your track record matters. **Keep track of your stats or KPIs (Key Performance Indicators), measure what matters (Objectives and Key Results), and you can be confident that your activity and processes will drive results. Process is the path to success.**

The Boston Celtics are one of the best franchises in sports, and they won the NBA championship in 2024. They have a young, sustainable core team under contract, and a lot of analysts think they are set up to be the next NBA dynasty. Their culture is all about process over results; it is a basketball version of *Moneyball*, where the entire organization prioritizes process over results. You can measure inputs more accurately than outputs. If you focus on process, the results will take care of themselves.

After the Celtics won the title, Brad Stevens, President of Basketball Operations, was asked, "What does this say about your team?" Stevens answered that the team had been doing the same things for years. They just happened to have won the championship in 2024. You can't control everything; they needed a little luck, some good breaks, and solid health in terms of the players not missing games. But the bottom line for the Celtics is that they had been working the same process for years.

Every business can learn from this kind of sustainable model. For that to happen, though, you need to realize that, as the leader, there's a difference between being *the* leader and *a* leader. *The* leader is in charge of making sure that all your other leaders are the right people in the right seats, doing the right things, making it happen—and if they're not, it's your fault. Your job is literally to hire and fire people, to correct inappropriate behavior, fix problems, and make sure everybody else is doing their job the right way. I like how Ben Horowitz's book *The Hard Thing About Hard Things* illustrates this perfectly. **If you're not willing to lean in, get your hands dirty, and have the hard conversations, then maybe**

leadership is not for you. If you combine that willingness to lead people with the accountability of key metrics, you will more than likely have a sustainable model.

THE CORE OF LEADERSHIP: INFLUENCING CHANGE AND INSPIRING GROWTH

Innovative and thoughtful strategies absolutely matter in the business world, but the heart of Executive Strategy is your mission, your vision, and your values. If these are off, if they aren't true, if they don't resonate—if they don't reflect who you are as a leader—then all the strategy in the world can't help you reach your full capacity. **The core of leadership comes from who you are as a person: leading by example, inspiring others, confronting change, displaying emotional intelligence, nurturing a culture of continuous learning, and building and sustaining a high-performance team of people who actually want to follow you.**

Leading by Example: The Cornerstone of Effective Leadership

As mentioned before, but worth repeating: You cannot lead your team somewhere you haven't been. You will never be the leader you need to be if you don't lead by example. Do the dirty work, show your people that you are in it with them, routinely get in the ditch and start digging next to the lowest person on the ladder. There is no replacement for this. **There is nothing more powerful, no secret to growing**

your business more important, than regularly being in the trenches working side by side with your team. If you don't do this, your chances of failing rise exponentially. But if you do, then it will become harder and harder to fail.

Inspirational Leadership: Motivating and Empowering Others

Your mission, vision, and values must be powerful enough to inspire others. When you share them with others, if they don't reply, "Wow, that is motivational and I am super excited about this," then it's likely that your mission, vision, and values are boring. Your vision should be so inspiring that when you talk about it, other people get excited just hearing it. Your

> **Your mission, vision, and values must be powerful enough to inspire others.**

primary job is to find the best people, motivate them with your vision, and empower them to be as great as they can be. A true CEO is in the people business; you are a leader of people, first and foremost. If you can't motivate your people, then you need to find someone who can. Remember, as we explored in previous chapters, that the start of this kind of inspirational leadership is listening, spending time with your people, and caring enough about their perspective to take their advice and try to do what they ask you to do. In other words, this kind of inspirational leadership is called "service." **Serve your people, and they will run through brick walls for the good of the team.**

Emotional Intelligence in Leadership

Serving your people well, listening and leading by example, and inspiring your team all require emotional intelligence. Cultivating emotional intelligence takes time, intentionality, and (for many leaders) actual training. Not everyone is born able to connect naturally and empathetically with others. This may be an area where you hire a consultant or take classes, but you should definitely reach out to people in your life who don't work for you and ask, "Would you say I'm emotionally intelligent, or is this an area where I need to grow?"

Without emotional intelligence, you will leave a wake of bodies, whether those are miserable team members, resignations and high turnover, or even litigants. Again, as a CEO, you are in the people business, and you need to understand people at least as well as you understand your product, market, and sales strategy. Do not underestimate the power of emotional connection and understanding.

Empathy is the number one skill that you need to develop as an emotionally intelligent leader. Sometimes it's hard for leaders to sit down, listen to someone's problems, and resist the urge to tell them to "suck it up." But putting yourself in others' shoes and understanding their problems, pain, and frustrations will grant you a better point of view when people share their frustrations. **One exercise in empathy is to repeat back to them the frustration they just shared and then ask, "How does that make you feel?" After they express how it made them feel, take the time to ask, "What were the effects of these feelings on you?" Then,** after listening to their fully thought-out feelings, ask, "Do you have any ideas on how to resolve these issues or how I can help?" By following this simple process, you will build better relationships with your team members, deepening your empathy skills and ultimately becoming a better leader.

SELLING IS THE LIFEBLOOD OF YOUR BUSINESS

You need to understand that nothing happens in your business until someone sells something. Assuming that your sales team, systems, and management are not vital to your success is foolhardy. The problem is that over time, the word "selling" has developed a bad reputation. Here are some of the best universal sales-success principles to build into your company culture around adopting the proper form of selling, while avoiding the term's negative connotations:

- The definition of selling is "helping someone get what they need or want."
- Closing is a service. It is simply helping someone get from point A to point B and make a decision faster.
- The best salespeople in the world are the best at asking questions and listening. The worst salespeople in the world talk too fast and make things up to just "get the sale."
- The best salespeople in the world have massive integrity; they do what they say and say what they do.

- Selling is a numbers game. The more people you see, the more people will buy.
- Identify someone's buying behavior and adapt your selling style to their decision-making style. Give driver decision makers options and let them feel in control. Give analytical decision makers stats and help them make a logical decision. Take it slow with collaborative decision makers and find ways to get others involved to help create consensus. And for emotional decision makers, make the buying experience fun and easy.
- People love to buy and hate to be sold.

Sales Leadership: Recruiting

A great leader is a great recruiter. Most problems in business can be solved by recruiting your way out of it. When a key person quits, or a negative person is bringing the team down, or you have someone who keeps making huge, costly mistakes . . . you recruit your way out of the problem. Developing recruiting skills will be valuable. You will help create your ideal company culture by recruiting the people who will represent your ideal culture. For key executive positions, the best team members are typically the ones who you recruit away from something else. Part of your job as a leader is to be constantly recruiting everywhere you go—the process is never-ending. As discussed in the Business Development section, **having a well-defined recruiting process constantly propels the business forward.**

Sales Leadership: Management

As a leader of salespeople, you need to understand that fear is the biggest obstacle your team will face. Fear of rejection, of the unknown, of success—they all come from the same place. As Tony Robbins says, "FEAR stands for False Evidence Appearing Real." Getting your sales team to overcome their fear and take action is how you cure the fear. It sounds simple but it's not.

The first thing you need to do as a leader is build rapport with each person on your sales team and discover their core motivations are. From there you need to help them create a vision for their life. **Part of the art of being a world-class sales leader is tying what you do as a company to each team member's vision for their life.** After establishing their life vision and purpose, you then help them set specific and measurable goals with a time frame, then reverse-engineer their goals down to daily activity. Write down these activity-based metrics and create a tracking tool so they can hold themselves accountable to the activity it takes to achieve their goals.

After this process, all you need to do is ask for permission to hold them accountable to their goals, then meet with them weekly to review the activity scorecard you helped them create. Ensure they are putting in the activity needed to achieve their goals. If they are falling short, simply say, "Remind me of

> Part of the art of being a world-class sales leader is tying what you do as a company to each team member's vision for their life.

your goals and why they are important for your life vision." Then after they tell you, say, "It looks like you need to change your goals and life vision." They will get upset and say, "No way!" To which you respond, "It's very simple. Your activity is in direct correlation to you achieving your goals. If you care about your goals, then you care about your activity every day. To have congruence you need to either change your goals or do more activity. What do you want to do?" And there you have it: You are now a world-class sales leader.

Last, remember that your team does not care how much you know until they know how much you care. **Your team spells "care" "T-I-M-E."** You have to invest time into your team to let them know you care about them. Not only do you need to schedule a one-on-one with them every week, every quarter you should spend a whole day with every direct report. As part of this agenda, take them to breakfast, lunch, or dinner. Also, try to do something personal with them at least once a year. Take them to a concert or go to a sporting event—the best is being invited to one of their kids' school plays or games! The more you invest into their emotional bank account, the more they will excel when you need them to turn up the volume on the sales effort to hit a big company goal.

CULTURE EATS STRATEGY FOR BREAKFAST: HOW TO CREATE A WORLD-CLASS CULTURE

As the leader, you are responsible for your corporate culture. Look around you, or even better, send out a survey that will answer the following questions:

- Are people having fun?
- Does the team love what they do for work?
- Does the team know the company's mission, vision, and values?
- Is the team living into the company's mission, vision, and values?
- Does the team have a 9-to-5 J-O-B? Or do they have a "whatever it takes to get the job done" job? In other words, does the team take ownership of the results for the company?
- Do people like to spend time together with each other outside of work?

Most people have experienced a toxic work culture. It typically starts with a toxic leader. If the leader is focused on controlling the company, and their objective is to maintain as much control and power in the company as possible, this is the catalyst for a toxic work culture. The telltale sign of a power-and-control leader is their decisions are based not on merit but on opinion. For example, if you hear of a leader terminating other leaders because of personality conflicts or—worse—firing key people with no explanation, then one can assume it is solely because the top leader wants them gone. Often a toxic leader will see an emerging leader outshining them, and to protect their legacy and reputation of power and control, they will get rid of the threat. This is the classic Mafia-style leadership: Kill your opponents before they become more powerful than you.

The opposite is healthy, empowering leadership. The best leaders create the best cultures. It starts with the leader being humble. Humble people are willing to share their power, delegate control, and coach others to grow them to a greater level than they can achieve on their own. The best cultures have an environment where people feel free, are passionate about what they do, and operate out of a strong desire to live into the mission, vision, and values of the company.

How to Create a World-Class Culture

Google is probably the best example of creating a world-class culture. In his book *In the Plex*, Steven Levy talks about how Google established the culture of only hiring the smartest and best engineers in the world, while investing in everything those people would need in order to have fun while at work. What's interesting was that Google, by creating a unique, cool, and fun culture with things like in-house private chefs making healthy high-end food, bicycles to ride around the campus, and games to play in the main lobby, became a place where people would work more and work harder—even though many leaders would've considered these amenities a distraction from work. People love to have the option to have fun, and the right people will want to perform while having fun.

How did Google do it? It's my first step to creating a world-class culture: They only hired the best. My good friend and business partner, Theo Davies, was Google's head of sales enablement for Asia. He's told me that getting a job at Google is harder than being accepted at an Ivy League school like Harvard. Google's hiring process is one that all companies should learn from. **The harder you make it for somebody to**

get a job with you, the more that they're going to want to be part of your company culture.

People draw their first impression of your company culture during the interview process. That is why your first step toward building a world-class culture should be to introduce job candidates to your culture by establishing a well-defined step-by-step interview process. Remember, in addition to the steps I outlined earlier, how I advised that part of the interview process should be spending a day with someone that personifies your culture? Along with showing the hardest aspects of that position and offering them the chance to sign up anyway, your new people also will see the type of work ethic, customer service, and attitude you expect of new hires. Over time, as you hire people who absorb the best aspects of your culture, those traits will spread by osmosis through your entire company.

The second thing that you need to do to have a world-class culture is to **realize that the culture starts with you as the leader. You must always be growing, always be learning, and remember that you are personifying your brand. The speed of the leader is the speed of the pack.** If you want to know if a company culture is growing and thriving, look at their financials. If revenue and profits are growing year over year, that is a healthy indicator that the leader is growing themselves and pushing the culture to the next level. However, if revenue and profits are declining yearly since that leader stepped into that position, they probably are a toxic leader and are corroding the culture. The numbers never lie. The numbers tell the story.

The company's numbers are thus a good barometer for

how positively you are affecting its culture. Set a goal each year for growing your team's happiness. One way to do that would be looking at their length of tenure at the company, comparing the members' salaries against the market rate of their positions. If they're making more than that rate for that position in your area, take pride in this fact. Also, periodically survey them on how the company can improve, and find ways to elicit continuous feedback for making the company better. Again, people don't care how much you know until they know how much you care. By your eliciting and implementing feedback, the team will see that they are influencing the company culture and buy in further.

Third and last, to create a world-class culture you have to make work fun. **You should make fun mandatory and ensure that everything that the company does has an element of fun to it.** Planning out your agenda for all your company meetings should be one of the most important things that you do as a leader. I remember meeting with one of the best leaders that I know, who was leading at a company I used to work with. I asked him what he thought the number one thing was that made him successful as a leader. He said, "Planning out a well-orchestrated agenda." What he meant by that was looking at what the team needs and creating an agenda specific to driving forward the production and well-being of the team with every meeting that they have. Such a detailed agenda should specify which speakers will address particular topics or team requirements, such as improving their knowledge base, motivation, positivity, problem solving, or technical/efficiency issues. Along with ensuring the content of your meetings and training are specific to what will improve people's performance, include testimonials from clients and happy team members on your meeting agendas. During lunches or breakout meetings, go around the table and ask questions so people can get to know each other. Host dinners outside of work and attend team-building events such as laser tag, bowling, or doing a ropes course. Or take the entire team to the beach or lake, or to go snow skiing, and simply have fun and bond together. These are the types of things that take your camaraderie the extra mile and create a corporate culture where people will want to stay forever.

Change and Uncertainty

You already know that your business will have to evolve over time to sustain itself, especially in today's world. **Your job as a leader is to embrace change, step out into uncertainty, and be willing to risk safety for growth.** I mention later the importance of embracing change in your personal life, but it's just as important to do so as a leader at work. Do not get stuck in your ways, and show your people how to be open, curious, and always looking for a better way to build.

Combined with the principles of leading by example and inspiring your team, staying open to change and uncertainty will enable you and your people to navigate murky waters together, with a sense of unity, rather than you having to drag people forward. **If your people trust you, they will follow you. If they know you care about them, and believe you will listen to them, then they will trust you.**

Nurturing a Culture of Continuous Learning and Innovation

Related to embracing change and leading by example, show people how to keep learning, keep growing, and never stop trying new things. **Incentivize learning, the acquisition of new knowledge and skills, and experimentation.** You are either learning or dying. Your business cannot grow if you are not leading your team into new knowledge, fresh data, and updated skills. The world moves too fast, and there is too much to know, to plateau at a certain level of knowledge and stay there.

Think about how you can help guide your people toward this kind of mindset, how you can practically nurture this kind of culture. Prizes? Scholarships? Awards? Promotions? Book clubs? There are dozens of ways to do this, but they are going to start with you. You will never regret inspiring your company to lean into innovation and continuous learning.

Building and Sustaining High-Performance Teams

Last—and this is probably obvious by now—to reach your Optimal Capacity as a leader, you have to realize that, ultimately, it's not about you. Or at least not *only* about you. Your company, business, or brand will live and die by the strength of your team. You cannot, by definition, be a successful CEO alone. **Leadership is about building the right kind of team by finding the right kind of people and then positioning them to be the best versions of themselves, together.** We've already covered the basics of building this kind of team, but it's crucial to remember the central role your team will play in the success or failure of everything you do. This is your reminder that you were never meant to do everything on your own, and that your ability to find people who are better than you at what they do will supercharge your capacity and reinforce your strengths while minimizing your weaknesses.

Leadership is hard, and it's not for everyone, but it also doesn't exist in a business-world vacuum. You are not a robot. To become the leader you were meant to be, you will need to find a strategic balance between the work, family, and personal arenas of your life. Each one of these aspects of who you are as a whole person feeds the others and increases your total capacity. In other words, to be a leader, **you have to be the kind of person people want to follow.**

STRATEGIC BALANCE: BUSINESS INNOVATION, FAMILY LIFE, AND PERSONAL GROWTH

It's one thing to strive for Optimal Capacity at work—it's the focus of this book—but for it to mean something, for it to matter, your work cannot be your life's only focus. In other words, **you have to grow your capacity for things other than your business if you want to live the best version of your life.** Your actual Optimal Capacity includes your business, personal growth, and family life, working in strategic balance.

If you don't have your health and you don't have your family and friends, then your career accomplishments can feel hollow. Show me one billionaire who can't walk and is stuck in a bed because of a heart attack or cancer who wouldn't trade all their money to be able to live another year. Someone who is on their deathbed because they didn't take care of their health is not operating at full capacity. In the same way, show me one billionaire who dies and has nobody come to their funeral but those who made money off of them—not even their family—and tell me that they are a success. Neither scenario is what anyone would call a good strategy.

You have to make balance a priority. **People like me who have a high capacity, who have the ability to work 80 to 100 hours a week without it fazing them, have to be intentional about scheduling time with the people they love.** To ensure you properly balance your time between work and life, operate by a set of rules, some of which follow.

First is the "6:00 pm Rule." Be home at 6:00 five out of seven nights a week, in time for dinner, no matter what. If there's one night a week where you have to take somebody out for an interview or work late, tell your partner. Setting these sorts of clear expectations with your spouse about how much you're working and making sure they're on the same page with you is paramount. You can do this exercise together. Start with a piece of paper and say, "Alright, what time am I going to be home? How many nights a week?"

Another important rule is called the "Three-Day Rule." We created this rule when my wife was pregnant with my daughter, Haven, 14 years ago. At the time, I was running an international coaching business and traveling to Europe all the time, and Kyah was concerned that I was going to be away running and building the business while she was stuck at home raising our daughter alone.

So, **we created a Three-Day Rule, which says that if I'm gone more than three days, Kyah and Haven come with me.** Over the last 13 years, more than 90% of the time when I've been gone for three days or more, Kyah and Haven have come along.

A positive by-product of that is that Haven, before the age of 10, had 30 different countries listed on her passport. She got this awesome life experience because our family time together is a priority. She can look back and say that as a kid she got to see the world, instead of growing up and saying, "My dad was never around."

Another important rule for me is **"Never stop dating your spouse."** Always prioritize having a weekly date night. I also try to have a monthly date night with my daughter. Now, I'm not perfect, but I think we do a pretty good job, and they definitely know those nights are a priority for me. We get it right more than we get it wrong.

Last, and this is more of an ironclad truth than a rule, **"You can't manage your family."** Your spouse and your kids are not compensated team members that you can fire. I know I've made that mistake, and I've had to learn this lesson the hard way. I would come home from having many people that report to me, who mostly listen to what I ask because I could fire them, then tell my wife or my daughter to do something, and they'd look at me like I was crazy.

While you cannot manage your family, leading your family does make you the ultimate leader at work, because what you do with your family helps you grow as a person. Do you lose your temper with them? Do you affirm them when they're doing things right? Do you do the little things—take out the trash, wash the dishes? Are you affectionate? The point is, **they're watching you way more than they're listening to what you're telling them to do,** and your team at work is too. I think that's where team members pick up resentment (though it manifests differently than it does for your family), because a team member might stick with you and have a smile on their face, both because they need the job and they actually get to leave you and go home. By contrast, your family will rebel against you if you try to manage them. **When things are dysfunctional at work or at home, understand as a leader that it's usually you that's the problem.**

RECHARGE: LESSONS FROM A CROSS-COUNTRY RV SABBATICAL

Okay, rules are great, but what does it actually look like to reach for full Optimal Capacity, for balance between work, personal growth, and family life? When I knew it was time to move on from a season in my life as one company's CEO, my family and I decided to recharge with a yearlong cross-country sabbatical. We made a plan, simplified our lives, got an RV, packed up, and hit the road.

The Educational Adventure: Road Schooling

Our RV journey corresponded with my daughter's fifth grade school year. We drove from Nashville down the entire Baja peninsula to San José del Cabo and back up the peninsula, and kept going all the way up to Spokane, Washington. Next, we drove from Spokane to Skaneateles, New York, on one of the Finger Lakes. We then headed back down to Nashville. All told, we made 42 stops in between, and we were gone almost a year.

We had pulled our daughter out of her private school, so I became the homeschool teacher for math. We would watch YouTube videos and do problems together. Kyah was the reading, English, and writing teacher, and for history we would visit places like the Al-

> When things are dysfunctional at work or at home, understand as a leader that it's usually you that's the problem.

amo. We would watch a movie about the Alamo, learn about it through watching, then physically go there, and Haven would remember everything, because she watched the movie before we went. That became a little hack when we traveled to various places. We would try to watch a movie about it, and then she would go into the museum or on the tour.

We did have a fear that she would be going into sixth grade behind the other kids, asking ourselves, "Is this a disservice?" But that's not what happened. When we got back to Nashville, she was ahead. She received an award at the end of the school year; she was number three in her entire class in math and number one in her English literature class, and she had some of the top grades in her entire class! She was one of the top three students in the entire sixth grade the year after we homeschooled her in an RV, driving across the country. It was amazing. She was put in all the honors classes for the next year. This all came from our desire to make family and personal growth a priority.

Adventure and Personal Development

What I've found is that because adventure requires risk, it's hard not to experience personal growth when you get out of your comfort zone and try old things (like school or family time) in completely new ways. After a year in an RV, Haven went from struggling to thriving; she had a much more developed sense of identity, she wasn't trying to impress anyone at school the next year, and her confidence went through the roof. It was a huge confidence-building experience, but it was more than that.

Atop the list of things Haven had been struggling with before the year of road schooling was identity. She had wanted so much to be one of the cool kids, and wasn't being accepted, which led to her struggle with confidence. Everything was tied together. But after investing significant amounts of time in the RV together, with us building her up, affirming and course-correcting her, she transformed into a completely new kid. So not only did Haven grow from our year of adventure, but so did Kyah and I—as parents, as teachers, and as a team. We're a stronger team now than we've ever been. Without taking that RV sabbatical, even though there were times it felt super risky, we wouldn't have experienced the growth we did.

Building Stronger Family Bonds

All of this—going on adventures together, dating your spouse, having date nights with your kids, knowing you can't "manage" your family—ties together. Knowing you are not the CEO of your family, but instead, learning how to best lead your family, helps you become a better leader at work, because you **know how to serve, care, listen better, and lead by example.** But the rewards at home for this kind of work are, in my opinion, way better than even the best days at work. And even when things don't go the way you'd planned or hoped, the personal growth and family bonds can transform even negative surprises into positive ones.

The Skiing Challenge and the Jeep Incident

For instance, we had a goal to ski 20 times during the RV year, since it's an activity we all love, it challenges us, and it helps bring us closer together. It was near the end of our trip—we had just finished skiing at Jackson Hole, and we were down to number 20, our final ski-challenge adventure. We were going over the continental divide between Wyoming and Montana, and all of a sudden, my Jeep's brakes caught on fire. I was going through the town of Ennis, Montana, when I realized it, and I had to jump out with my wife and several water jugs. Flames were literally shooting out of the brakes of our Jeep. It was completely toast. They had just had a blizzard in Ennis, so everything was completely shut down, covered in snow. We had to get the police to come help us push the car into a coffee shop parking lot. Then we had to go park at the nearest RV park in Ennis.

Again, I think it's not what happens to you in life, but how you respond to it that matters, and my initial response was to be pissed off and super frustrated. My first thought was, "Crap. Now we're not going to hit our goal of skiing 20 times in a year." I was so locked in on that, that it took me a minute to realize, "Wait, we're stuck in this really cool town in Montana, and I'm sure there's cool things we can do." For instance, my brother-in-law called me and let me know that Ennis is one of the best fly fishing spots in America. After realizing this, I was able to go get a fishing guide and have an amazing fishing day on one of the days we were stuck there.

But the coolest thing about that "detour" was that we fired up our Starlink satellite connection and plugged into a new-to-us TV series called *The Chosen*, which we binge-watched as a family. It was one of the most amazing family-bonding experiences we've ever had. I cried during almost every episode, and my daughter learned the Bible from a different perspective. Watching that as a family was a great experience, and we never would have carved out that much time if we hadn't broken down in the middle of nowhere.

GROWING YOUR PERSONAL CAPACITY

The reality of balancing work, family, and personal growth is that while all three feed into each other, personal growth—who you are becoming at the core of your being—is the most crucial aspect of strategic balance, influencing the other two areas at least as much as they influence personal growth, if not more. Work can be a healthy part of your identity, and so can your family life, but something deeper has to be feeding those areas for you to reach Optimal Capacity as a whole person. **I've learned that overcoming challenges, lifelong learning, embracing flexibility, being present, cultivating personal interests, balancing ambition and contentment, and aligning with a higher purpose are some of the most important things we can do that increase our capacity in every area of our lives.**

Overcoming Challenges and Building Resilience

We have all heard: It's not what happens to you, it's how you respond to it that matters. This comprises your character. **You don't know what your character really is until it's tested.** Anybody can have a positive attitude, keep a smile on their face, and say positive things to you when times are good and there's nothing crazy happening in their life. But when life gets tough, everything goes wrong, people wrong you, you're being attacked or persecuted, you experience trials of any kind, that's where your character is revealed.

Our posture should always be one that boasts of the goodness of God, especially when we feel like we are crushing it at life. It's easy for our pride to let us believe that we are crushing it because we are doing so many things well. That we are strategically at the top of our game. But a humble reliance on God when we realize that it's by his grace that we move through this world, using the talents he's given each of us, to maximize our love and capacity for serving others, develops the spiritual muscle that we need. When challenges and hardships inevitably come, we are no stranger to relying on God to carry us through them. 2 Corinthians 12:9–10 (English Standard Version) reads, "But he said to me, 'My grace is sufficient for you, for my power is made perfect in weakness.' Therefore I will boast all the more gladly of my weaknesses, so that the power of Christ may rest upon me. For the sake of Christ, then, I am content with weaknesses, insults, hardships, persecutions, and calamities. For when I am weak, then I am strong." The Bible talks about God being with you in your weakness and at the lowest times. The real exercise here is understanding that even at the best of times and at the worst of times, God's grace is sufficient. So God gets the glory for the wins, and he carries, refines, and prepares us in the middle of life's storms. These seasons of refinement are beautiful and necessary and life changing when met with humility. I've certainly had my hard seasons, and I've learned such valuable lessons during those times, and by God's grace have come through them. I count those seasons as some of the most precious times because in my weakness, God was glorified. Regardless of where you stand on faith, I've found it to be the foundation on which all my pillars find their footing.

> It's not what happens to you, it's how you respond to it that matters.

Now, failing, that's a completely different thing than losing. People fail all the time. It's quitting, though, and giving up when times get hard, when life deals you a bad hand, when somebody persecutes you, giving up when you hit rock bottom, that's when you lose. It's all about having your identity on solid ground, which we are going to dive into a bit more a few sections from now.

Lifelong Learning and Continuous Improvement

If you're not learning, you're dying. At least that's what Albert Einstein thought. Jim Rohn said it, too: Never stop learning. As soon as you think you know it all, that's the beginning of the end.

One of the most exciting things about life is learning new things, experiencing new challenges. A leader is a reader. A leader is a learner, and to think otherwise is arrogant. And there are a lot of arrogant leaders out there who hit a certain level of knowledge, then consider themselves the ultimate source of wisdom. But if you stop learning, it will catch up to you.

In order to stay a learner, and to be a constant, never-ending student, you have to have the humility to say, "I do not know it all." I think it's scary for somebody to say they know it all. Here is a great perspective: "The more that I know, the more I know that I don't know." When I become a kind of expert at something, if I know close to everything about a very, very narrow topic, that makes me very aware of how much I don't know about everything else. Then, I use that as a kind of fuel or motivation to want to learn more and expand my horizons.

Try to take that same attitude toward many different things in your life, to keep learning about as many different things as you can, versus getting complacent and saying, "I already know enough. I don't need to read another book." We are never too rich, or too accomplished, or too seasoned to stop learning new things.

Embracing Flexibility and Adaptability

Life has a way of punishing you for being too rigid. Hold things loosely, so you don't kill yourself white-knuckling everything all the time. If you can't let go of anything, you'll eventually break under that weight. Tom Brady was the greatest quarterback who ever played in the NFL, and he had a longer career than anyone thought he could have. One huge reason for that is that, years into his career, he started to focus on plyometrics, which is all about flexibility and being able to absorb force while staying loose.

In high school, wrestling was that way for me. The harder I would try, the stiffer I was; the more I was overthinking, focusing on technique, the more I would get beat. But as soon as I let all that go, and decided, "I am not going to think about what I'm doing when I'm on the mat. I'm in the flow. I'm giving it everything I've got," suddenly, I became one of the best wrestlers in the state.

Selling is the same way. As I mentioned earlier, **people love to buy, but they hate to be sold.** If you're intentionally thinking, "I am selling you right now," they will not buy. But if you think, "I'm just going to go have a nice conversation with this person," then their perception will be completely different and they'll buy all day long.

And life is, in general, that same way. The people that try

too hard in life, who can't change gears, are kind of hard to be around. It is hard to have the energy to be around someone that's wound up all the time, but the person that's relaxed, going with the flow, not forcing things to happen all the time—that's who people want to be around.

That's how Harrison Ford got the role of Han Solo in *Star Wars*. He wasn't asked to audition for the role, and in fact he was kind of pissed that George Lucas didn't ask him to be in the movie, because they were friends. But then one day, Lucas brought in Carrie Fisher to audition for Princess Leia, and the guy who was supposed to read lines with her wasn't there, so they asked Ford to do it, because he was just doing some carpentry around the set as his side gig, not having "made it" as an actor yet. He just had a laissez-faire attitude; he was like, "Whatever, Princess." And in watching him read, the *Star Wars* people said, "Yeah, that's it. That's Han Solo." Because Ford was just "whatever" about it. And that was Han Solo. The people casting the movie thought he was perfect. That reading launched his whole career. Whatever the opposite of "desperate" was, that was Harrison Ford that day, and that's why he became Han Solo.

For me, getting into my flow state ties back to my spiritual journey, and belief in God. **If you actually trust God, that He has the best things for you, then you don't have to force it to happen.** You can say, "I have done everything I can. I've made the best decisions I could with the information I had at the time. I've put in the effort, and the results are up to God. So, if this is gonna happen, it's gonna happen. I don't have to worry about it." That is the ultimate flexibility, and it allows you to adapt to any situation. That kind of faith is the opposite of control, and it allows you to embrace change in every area of your life. You can be open to whatever comes your way, because it doesn't have to perfectly fit your preconceived notions.

Mindfulness and Presence

Being truly present is extremely important. **When you talk to someone, no matter what else is going on, they need to be the only person you are focused on.** You want to be the type of present leader that when people are talking with you, and there's 100 people in the room, and you just walked off stage, or you have five other meetings right after, you are still absolutely present. Every time people meet with you, they feel like they are the only person that exists. That kind of mindful presence is something people remember.

This is the ultimate leadership quality, and it means letting go of your ego. Many highly driven people are always thinking of the next thing. **It takes self-discipline to force your mind not to go to the next thing, to let go of whatever might happen next and focus on the now.**

What if this building explodes and there is no next hour? What if it's the end of the world? Dramatic, yes, but we don't know what's going to happen tomorrow, or even in the next hour. But what I do know is I have this human in front of me right now who needs me for something. That's all I've got. This is what is real. There is nothing besides myself and the person who needs my attention. It's a practice, like prayer, and what some people call "mindfulness." It's not automatic, but it's worth working at.

Cultivating Personal Interests

Life is too short to not have fun. Why in the world would you only work and not have fun with the resources that you're creating from working so hard? Don't wait for retirement to do what you envision doing. Years back, I was in the second year of launching my first company when I happened to see a YouTube video. At the time, I was easily working 100 hours a week. My wife informed me around this time that we'd been married for two years and hadn't taken a vacation yet.

At the time I watched this YouTube video, I was in my twenties, and the guy who made the video was probably in his mid-forties. And he said that he created this vision for his life, that he had a list of all the things that he wanted to do when he retired, but that he was going to do them now. He would actually take an entire month off each year and go on these amazing adventures with his family or his friends every year.

He told the story of the first time he did it. He was super nervous, because, you know, when you're leading a business and fires are popping up every day, you think that when you leave, you'll come back and the company won't exist anymore. But the reality is, if you've set things up the right way, you've hired the right team, and you've done everything you're supposed to do, then when you come back, everything and everyone will still be there. Sometimes things happen despite you, like they sold something or solved a difficult problem while you were gone. And then you just pick it back up. When you take time for yourself, you are ten times more effective and efficient as a leader after you've recharged your batteries than when you are being a workaholic.

Some examples of fun hobbies are fly fishing, snow skiing, yoga, guys' trips, and family trips, which are really helpful when it comes to recharging. Our family goes to Cabo, Mexico, for two weeks each July, nine years in a row so far. Those kinds of traditions are powerful. Similarly, a long time ago, my dad started a family tradition with my brothers and me, and this year will be the 39th year in a row of the Hillis boys' annual fishing trip. When it comes to skiing, we buy passes, and every year we do two ski trips with another family as a joint tradition. It enriches your life to have these adventures as a family. They don't have to be expensive hobbies or traditions, but it can be camping or an annual excursion. Traditions that involve down time and conversation and movement. Having hobbies and traditions rounds you out as a person. When you go to dinner, this gives you interesting topics to talk to people about. You can discuss more than just work and find common interests.

And people want that. People don't want you to be a corporate drone who doesn't have a life. It's not inspiring for other team members. Think of it this way: **Most people want to work with you as their leader because they see something in you or in your life that they want to aspire to.** If all you do is work, not many people out there will look at a workaholic and say, "Wow, I really want to grow up and be a workaholic." People will be drawn to your team if they see you living a life that is both productive and enjoyable.

On that note, your social media should reflect all the facets of your life. The work, the passion projects, the charitable organizations you want to amplify, and the hobbies and travel you enjoy. The right team members will want to be a part of that culture and appreciate getting to know who they are working with. As with all things, common sense should be applied to social media content, but I've found social media to be a great recruiting tool, and people often reach out to inquire about positions with companies I've led because of social media content.

Balancing Ambition with Contentment

Another way to think about this kind of human balance is to pursue a balance of ambition with contentment. You can be one of the most driven people ever, but without contentment, life feels like one thing after another. Always keep striving, but if you never stop to enjoy what you've been given, what you've built, life feels a little one-dimensional and flat.

You can make a lot of money, get complacent, and retire, but to be honest I don't think that's any better than being a workaholic. I heard Rabbi Daniel Lappin speak about this once. He said two interesting things. One was, in the Hebrew language, the word "retirement" doesn't exist. The second was how they define the word "work": **work in Jewish communities is defined as fulfilling a need in society**. They think that retiring is simply a disservice to society, because if your work is filling a societal need, then that's your purpose. If you're filling a need, then retirement isn't an option! You're needed! That was really impactful for me. It's how I've framed my thoughts ever since about why I work. I'm actually filling a need in society.

It's worth asking the question: "**What has God called you to do in the world?**" Viewed this way, work is not work. You don't even feel like you're working. If you don't have a purpose—or if you're complacent—and you're doing things just to make money, look at yourself in the mirror and ask, "**Is this fulfilling my purpose in life?** Am I actually happy?"

Because very rarely are people who are only working for money or status happy. Finding joy and fulfillment doesn't come from money, and it doesn't come from being on vacation 24/7. If that's your goal, congratulations. Go sit on the beach and do nothing. However, it really does take a balance. There are seasons to go all in, to let your ambition and your purpose push you to the limits of your capacity, and there are seasons to sit back, relax, and enjoy what you have.

Aligning with a Higher Purpose

As mentioned earlier, **having a foundation for who you are, your identity, and knowing yourself is critical.** If you are going to try crazy things, fail, and keep going, you have to know you have an unshakable foundation. A firm foundation is critical. Not politics, not your job title, not your company, not even your spouse or your kids . . . as sources of identity, these things and even people will occasionally let you down.

For me, my foundation is rooted in Christ. **If my identity wasn't in Christ, then there's no way I would have done all of the good things I've done.** The confidence that I've had to go out there and not only to start doing what I've done, but then to keep going, is purely rooted in who I know I am in Jesus. If your identity is in anything less solid than how God

sees you, then your foot is not on solid ground, and you will
be let down. You will be heartbroken. You will want to quit,
and you probably will, because everything else is finite. And
if you put your identity in politics, a company, some job title,
your boss, your spouse, your kids—all of those things will let
you down at some point in your life. And in my experience,
the only person who won't let you down is Jesus Christ.

THE WISDOM OF THE PILLARS: MAXIMIZING YOUR PERSONAL AND PROFESSIONAL CAPACITY

wrote this book to help you increase your capacity and build your business bigger than yourself. Executive Strategy and the other core Pillars will turn your entrepreneurial vision into a bridge to becoming a true CEO. Whether it is setting goals and aligning teams, or balancing your personal growth and family life, this book is meant to be a field guide you can return to again and again. Life comes at you fast, so embracing change and fostering innovation have to be paired with a set of core strategies and timeless truths that you can build on.

Remember that being a CEO is about leadership, and leadership is about influencing and inspiring others through listening, learning, and service. Who you are as a whole person will translate into how you lead and empower others. You are in the people business. Building people up creates the ultimate capacity. Your direct reports are an extension of you. You should constantly be teaching others how to do everything except the things only you can do. Spend all your time doing things that only you can do. You should constantly elevate your skills and abilities, take on personal projects of learning about new capabilities for your company, and then work toward delegating your old tasks to someone you've been mentoring.

A leader's job is to always be recruiting. Every problem that you have typically can be solved by recruiting somebody to help solve it. Growing a business bigger than what you can do alone means you are finding ways to get yourself out of being the person the business relies on to function, and hiring A+ people to whom you can delegate roles and responsibilities to run the business without you. Then you can invest your time building the business at the highest level strategically.

> Building people up creates the ultimate capacity.

Last, everything you build comes from who you are, so ensure that you've built your identity on a better foundation than work, money, or status. What is your identity? I had a leader once tell me, "My entire life identity is built around this company. My goal in life is to die working." That is sad. Life is so much more than what you do for work. You are a spiritual being composed of a spirit, body, community, family, friends, and vocation. Pouring your entire identity into work creates such an unhealthy balance that you end up being less effective there. Workaholics often find the opposite of what they were striving toward happening: They become less productive, less inspired by allowing their work to consume their entire life, and burn out. You were designed to be a whole person and a contributing member of society. Your family needs you. Your community needs you. Your friends need you. You need to take care of yourself. And yes, your work needs you ... but not all of you.

Last, every risk you take, every new place you lead your team, and every time you get up off the floor of failure, you need to know who you are, and who you belong to. All the 12-step programs and many top-performance leadership coaches recommend drawing your identity from a higher power, not just trying to rely on yourself. As I mentioned, that secure foundation is my relationship with God, my faith in who He says I am, and my identity in Jesus Christ, who has never let me down. That's the most important thing I have to give you: **the unshakable truth that no matter who you are or what you do, Jesus Christ is the only person who will never let you down and is the only provider of unlimited capacity.**

Acknowledgments

Thank you to the world-class team that made this book possible!

Thank you to my OG editor who helped me write the first manuscript, Ryan Huber.

Thank you to my agent, Esther Fedorkevich, for believing in me and getting me a seat at the bigger table with BenBella Books.

Thank you to Matt Holt for investing in and believing in me and this book being able to help people all over the world to create more capacity and build businesses bigger than themselves!

Notes

1. Blake Montgomery and Callum Jones, "WeWork, Once a $47bn Firm, Files for Bankruptcy After Accruing $2.9bn Debt," *The Guardian*, November 6, 2023, https://www.theguardian.com/business/2023/nov/06/wework-bankruptcy-debt-remote-work.

2. "Our Purpose," Chick-fil-A website, accessed June 6, 2025, https://www.chick-fil-a.com/careers/culture.

3. Kerry Patterson, Joseph Grenny, Ron McMillan, and Al Switzler, *Crucial Conversations: Tools for Talking When Stakes Are High*, 2nd ed. (McGraw Hill, 2012).

4. "The Collapse of Webvan; A $6 Billion Grocery Delivery Startup," *Bit of Business* (blog), January 18, 2021, https://www.bitofbusiness.com/post/collapse-of-webvan.

5. Dominick Reuter, "How Costco Became the King of Bulk Buying Starting Out Selling Only to Businesses Out of an Old Airplane Hangar," *Business Insider*, July 9, 2024, https://www.businessinsider.com/founding-history-of-costco.

Index

About the Author

Dustin Hillis is the founder of All Things New Ventures, a sweat equity business. He currently has three equity partners, including Tough Stump Technologies, a top military drone technology business; and Totally Mushrooms, a vertically integrated, upcycled mushroom technology farming and distribution business. Hillis's main focus today is his newest equity partner, SafeSpace Global Corporation (www.safespaceglobal.ai), where he is president and chief strategy officer. SafeSpace Global carries out its vision to be the global leader in ambient AI technology with a mission to help save lives. It is a publicly traded company on the OTC market (stock ticker SSGC).

Prior to launching All Things New Ventures, Hillis served 20 years at the Southwestern Family of Companies, founded in 1855. He also led the global conglomerate as CEO for four years, taking it from a loss to above forecast profit. Hillis was responsible for 20 diverse international businesses with over 20 presidents and CFOs as direct reports, who were responsible for over two thousand people worldwide. He led the way through several mergers and acquisitions and successfully sold and started several businesses.

In 2021, Hillis was recognized by *Industry Era* as a "Top 10 CEO." During his tenure as CEO, Hillis led many businesses, including a financial advising firm; four different insurance companies (two in Eastern Europe and two in the United States); companies engaged in executive search, real estate, luxury travel, international work exchange, international consulting, executive coaching, and training and keynote speaking; several direct-sales businesses in Europe; and the United States's oldest direct-sales business.

His experience as the cofounder of Southwestern Consulting and president of Southwestern Coaching (an international consulting and coaching business) earned him a "Top 50 Consulting Firm CEOs" distinction from *The Consulting Report.*

For more information about Dustin Hillis
and any of his companies mentioned in the book,
go to www.dustinhillis.com.